MAZES AND LABYRINTHS

A BOOK OF PUZZLES

By WALTER SHEPHERD

REVISED EDITION

DOVER PUBLICATIONS, INC., NEW YORK

Published in Canada by General Publishing Company, Ltd.,
30 Lesmill Road, Don Mills, Toronto, Ontario.

Published in the United Kingdom by Constable and Company, Ltd.,
10 Orange Street, London WC 2.

This Dover edition, first published in 1961, is a revised
version of the work originally published in 1942 by Penguin
Books Limited under the title *For Amazement Only*.

Standard Book Number: 486-20731-5

Library of Congress Catalog Card Number: 61-1683

Manufactured in the United States of America

DOVER PUBLICATIONS, INC.
180 Varick Street
New York, N. Y. 10014

CONTENTS

LET'S GO A-MAZING

THE oldest of all devices for the pleasure (and torture) of mankind is the labyrinth. Its origin is legendary, but the maze has always held a peculiar and persistent fascination for the human mind. There have been maze-fashions — crazes in mazes — separated by long periods in which they appear to have been forgotten except as curiosities, yet they have always cropped up again, sooner or later, with all their old power of appeal.

It is true that children alone care to spend their time in getting to the centre of a shapeless maze of lines by the laborious method of "trial and error," but there is much more in the modern idea of a maze-puzzle than that. Nevertheless, a harmoniously constructed labyrinth of lines may possess truly remarkable aesthetic charm, even when there is but one inevitable path to its centre. It is a matter for wonder, indeed, that of all the particular mazes ever designed the only one to be remembered without effort and with perpetual delight is a maze of this sort — the traditional maze of Dedalus. Here is a plan of it (Fig. 1) according to a worn incision on the southern wall of the porch of Lucca Cathedral, together with a translation of the Latin words inscribed beneath it.

According to the legend, Dedalus built the labyrinth at Cnossus to house the terrible bull-headed man, the Minotaur. Every nine years King Minos of Crete extorted a tribute of seven youths and seven maidens from the city of Athens, and cast them to the Minotaur to avenge his son. They sailed for Crete in a vessel with a black flag, and one day Theseus, son of the King of Athens, became a passenger on the tribute ship, and tracked the Minotaur to its lair and slew it. He made sure of his own escape by taking into the maze a thread given him by Ariadne (as we generally, but less prettily, spell her name), but if this was the maze of Dedalus he need not have bothered. There is only one path, and it is impossible to go wrong.

Yet it is a beautiful maze, and though only legendary* it is remembered before even the cruel maze which the twelve Egyptian kings built near Lake Moeris, and which was described by Herodotus. This frightful labyrinth had two stories, the upper for men and the lower for crocodiles. There is no doubt of its authenticity, for though its foundations were laid four and a quarter millenniums ago they were unearthed by Flinders Petrie in comparatively recent times.

* Some say that the Cretan labyrinth was the Palace of King Minos at Cnossus, whose ruins have been examined, but if so it was a labyrinth fitted with waterpipes and bathrooms. The Palace was destroyed about 1400 B.C., and passed from the knowledge of common men, but the legend of the labyrinth remains.

Fig. 1.   This is the labyrinth which the Cretan Dedalus built,
Out of which nobody could get who was inside,
Except Theseus; nor could he have done it,
Unless he had been helped with a thread by
Adriane, all for love.

Plans of the Egyptian maze are in existence, and they are not beautiful. There is no particular reason why *they* should be remembered, but the maze of Dedalus so fascinated the Cretans that they stamped it on their coins, sometimes giving it circular coils and sometimes rectangular ones. In Fig. 2 are two such coins, struck at Cnossus, and Fig. 3 shows

Fig. 2.   Cretan gold coins bearing the maze of Dedalus

the corresponding versions of the still popular "Greek fret," or "Greek key," ornament, which was devised in ancient times to perpetuate the labyrinthine pattern.

Fig. 3.   Labyrinthine decoration

In the ninth century the Christian emperors began wearing robes ornamented with mazes, and in the succeeding Ages of Ecclesiastical

Ingenuity, the Church found in the maze an object-lesson for the pilgrims of this perplexing world. They made labyrinths in mosaic work, so that penitents could laboriously trace out the path to "Ciel," and numerous churches were decorated with such designs. The maze at Lucca is a small example, but the traditional head of the Minotaur in the centre has long since been worn away by the tracing fingers of countless visitors.

Most of the church mazes are identical with this one in design, though they vary enormously in size and shape. That in the nave of the parish church of St. Quentin is octagonal, and measures $34\frac{1}{2}$ feet in diameter, while the circular maze at Chartres is 40 feet across. The maze at the church of St. Bertin, at St. Omer, is provided with "stations" for pilgrims, and to thread it was considered a sufficient substitute for an actual journey to the Holy Land. The octagonal maze at Amiens Cathedral was dated 1288, and was 42 feet across, but unfortunately it was destroyed in 1708.

Numerous other examples could be cited from the Continent, where they are known as *chemins de Jerusalem*, and in Problem No. 25 we give a medieval improvement on the traditional maze of Dedalus. Though it may actually be far older than our first record of it, it must surely have taken a churchman to devise so diabolical a maze as this! Here are beauty and treachery together, and the chief interest of it, to us, is to see the cunning of its structure. This is the only historical curiosity included in these problems, unless the "Philadelphia Maze" (No. 48) be admitted to the dignity of history.

In England, most of the older mazes are to be found out of doors in the neighbourhood of churches, but they seem to have been regarded as sources of amusement rather than as means of penance or pilgrimage. Many of them were mere ditches cut in the turf of a hill-top, and

FIG. 4.   THE "MIZ-MAZE," ST. CATHERINE'S HILL

such is the maze said to have been made by a college boy on St. Catherine's Hill, Winchester. This maze — known locally as the "Mizmaze"— may still be visited, and its plan is shown in Fig. 4. It measures 86 feet across, and its path is 600 yards long.

Variants of the old maze of Dedalus were cut in the turf at Alkborough in Lincolnshire, Wing in Rutlandshire, and numerous other places, some being given spiral centres. The mazes on Ripon Common

FIG. 5. THE MAZE AT BOUGHTON GREEN

and at Boughton Green, Nottinghamshire (shown in Fig. 5), are of this kind. Others were elaborated to include four or more "stations," like the maze at Saffron Walden and the one at Sneinton, Nottingham-

FIG. 6. THE MAZE AT SNEINTON, NOTTS

shire, given in Fig. 6. Village mazes were once very common in Dorsetshire, but most of them have vanished through neglect, and

> The nine men's morris is filled up with mud,
> And the quaint mazes in the wanton green
> For lack of tread are undistinguishable.
> —*A Midsummer Night's Dream*

The village mazes were often called "shepherd's races," "Julian's bowers" (St. Julian being the patron saint of tramps), or "mize-mazes" ("miz-mazes" in Hampshire and the West Country), and the one at Pimperne portrays the tortuous path of the pilgrims — of Love. We give it in Fig. 7, where it will be seen that its shape is an inverted heart. Other mazes in Dorsetshire are to be found at Leigh and Troy Town, and the word "troy-town" is itself sometimes used for "maze."

In the seventeenth century the garden-maze became fashionable, and an obsolete one at South Kensington is shown in Fig. 8. Such

FIG. 7.   THE PIMPERNE MAZE   FIG. 8.   KENSINGTON MAZE

mazes usually consist of seven-foot hedges, but occasionally trellis work is used, so that the visitors can see one another scratching their heads in the next passage. The most famous maze of this sort is undoubtedly the one built at Hampton Court in 1690 for the amusement of William III; it may still be visited, and is shown in Fig. 9 . According to Muir-head, in an authoritative guide to London, the clue to this maze is "to

FIG. 9.   HAMPTON COURT MAZE

turn to the right on the first and second occasions that we have a choice, and thereafter to the left," and this is true if you turn to the left immediately on entering the maze — which the present position of the turnstiles obliges you to do. But, after entering, an even better clue is simply to keep turning to the right whenever possible.

Figures 10 and 11 show two more garden-mazes, that at Theobalds consisting of a forced path and presenting no problem. The small German maze in Fig. 12 is given by the late Mr. H. E. Dudeney in his book, *Amusements in Mathematics*, which we hasten to acknowledge as our source of both this and the solution to the "Philadelphia Maze" given on page 118.

FIG. 10.   THE MAZE AT HATFIELD HOUSE, HERTFORDSHIRE

You may find fun or exasperation in wandering round the paths of such puzzle-gardens, and the chances are that you would merely be bored by running over the plans of them with a pencil. The problems in this book are not of that simple kind, though sometimes it will be found advisable to use a pointer of some sort.

FIG. 11.   THE MAZE AT THEOBALDS, HERTS

A matchstick or a long pin is better than a pencil, which spoils the page for the next comer, but if very light pencil lines *do* make their appearance, here and there, they may be erased with soft india-rubber. The use of tracing-paper, of course, leaves the book completely unmarked and allows you to make unlimited attempts without confusion. In Puzzle No. 37 it is expressly forbidden to use a pointer at all, the object of the maze being to test the use of the eye, its only traps consisting of optical illusions. And you will get more fun out of such problems as No. 26 by using the unaided eye. Other suggestions and devices are described at appropriate places in the text.

Many of these problems are not obviously maze-puzzles at all, but their claim to inclusion with the rest is the fact that they do involve wandering about the multitudinous rooms of castles and mansions. The very first problem is a simple and easy specimen of this sort. Mazes such as Nos. 22 and 28 may appear at first sight to be variants of the common or garden maze, but the problems set beside them are generally of quite a different nature.

FIG. 12. A GERMAN MAZE

Others, which still seem to be mere labyrinths, will be found to contain curious tricks for you to overcome, and in some cases the problem is to thread the maze within a given time-limit, for there is neither enjoyment nor merit in doggedly following every track till the right one is stumbled upon. Even crossword puzzles can be solved that way, given a large enough dictionary and a dull enough mind. In nearly all cases the solutions given are the only ones possible, but in one or two puzzles small variations are possible. This is not thought to matter.

The maze-puzzle performs a peculiar function in recreation. It becomes curiously acceptable at times when the mind is active but incapable of coherent reading. There seems to be something hypnotically soothing in the even lines and sweeping curves of a maze, and when your nerves cry out for activity but your eye is tired of type you may find, as others do, that to go a-mazing is the very best thing you can do. You may not have far to go. . .!

No. I
THE HALL OF SEVENTY ROOMS

Abou Ben 'Ad 'Em (may his tribe decrease!) determined to rob the Great Mogul, Arfamo, who kept the bulk of his riches in the Hall of Seventy Rooms. Each of these rooms, excepting only those against the outside walls, had four doors, and out of the one hundred and twenty-three doors fifty were always kept locked. Abou succeeded by a trick in drugging the guard, but his drugs, being of Foreign Manufacture, were not very good, and he had to find his way to the Treasure-Chamber through the open doors, and make his return journey, in something under five minutes.

Which way did he go?

Note: Abou did not use a pencil, so why should you?

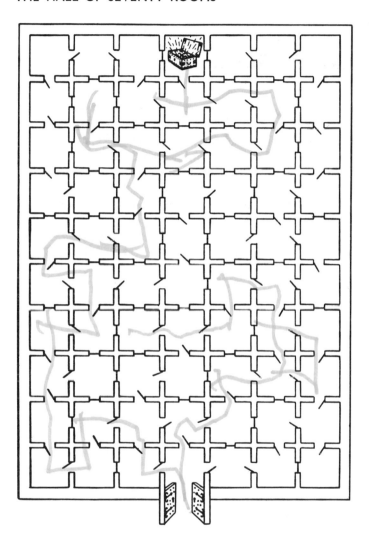

No. I

Easy

No. 2
A TANGLED TALE

Engineer Egbert had the misfortune to fall into enemy hands and was thrown into a concentration camp. Fortunately he had a small pair of wire-cutters behind his ear at the time, and these having been overlooked in the search for weapons, he resolved to make his escape through the barbed-wire entanglements at the earliest opportunity. Bought at Worthwhile's Stores for a very modest sum, these cutters were capable of making only six cuts, but Engineer Egbert succeeded in getting through the wire before they broke.

Starting at the top of the page, see if you can discover the six cuts which allowed Egbert to make his escape at the bottom.

Reminder: Use a pin instead.

No. 2

Medium

No. 3
THE GOLDEN APPLE

Not the least of the labours of Hercules was to obtain possession of the Golden Apples in the Garden of the Hesperides. They were protected by the dragon, Ladon, but an even greater obstacle was presented by the frailty of the apple-trees. A 200-pound man may easily kill a dragon, but he may not climb a tree to the height of a rook's nest without risk. Yet Hercules got this apple from the very top of the tree.

To find the way Hercules climbed the tree, start at the bottom of the trunk and ascend the branches, but you may not cross a line.

Answer to correspondent: Yes, Daisy, by all means use a hat-pin.

No. 3

Easy

No. 4

SCISSORS CUT PAPER

If you travel by train in China you may often see people passing the time with what looks like a deaf-and-dumb conversation. They thrust clenched fists and open palms into each other's faces with astonishing rapidity, but they are not talking — they are playing "Scissors Cut Paper." Two fingers held apart represent a pair of scissors, an open palm a sheet of paper, and a closed fist a stone. If your opponent offers you a fist, you must reply with a palm, for "paper wraps stone." A palm must be answered with two fingers, for "scissors cut paper." Two fingers must be met by a closed fist, for none will deny that a "stone blunts scissors."

Beginning at the top left-hand corner, see if you can make your way to the bottom right-hand corner without hesitation. You may move from square to square vertically, horizontally, or diagonally, as long as you preserve the order — scissors, paper, stone, scissors, etc. In the Solutions we give the *shortest* way only, so count your moves. Also, guess without counting the number of stones, pieces of paper, and pairs of scissors in the diagram.

Note: There's not much point in a pencil this time, is there?

No. 4

Easy

No. 5
CATCHING THE ADDER

Brusher Mills was a famous character in the New Forest, England, half a century ago. His job was to catch snakes, and he used to supply the Zoo with upwards of two hundred a year for feeding to the hamadryads. He used to catch his adders with his finger and thumb, seizing them by the neck or tail and dropping them into a sack.

Here is a nest of adders, one of which is showing his head. This adder's tail is one of the three on the circumference of the circle, but before you seize it you must make sure it is the right one. If you take hold of the wrong tail, an unsuspected head may pop out somewhere and give you a bite.

Warning: Adders have a strong objection to being poked or scratched with a pencil. Better follow their coils by eye.

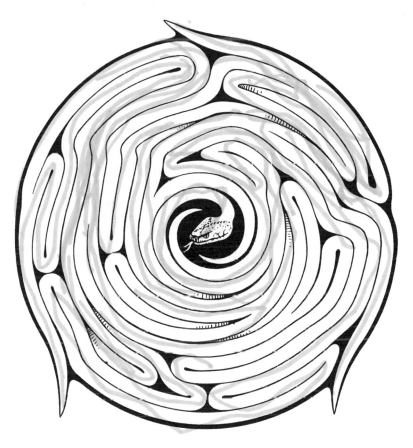

No. 5

Easy

No. 6

ALLEY BARBER AND THE THIRTY THUGS

Resolved to rescue the maiden in the pot of hot oil at the top right-hand corner of the diagram, Alley Barber fearlessly entered the secret maze of gangster Harry Al Rancid. He passed the tree at the bottom, on the left, but soon discovered that the maze was full of thugs armed with hammers. Giant though he was, Alley Barber had sufficient strength to tackle only two of them, and he actually managed to reach the maiden without meeting more than the prescribed couple.

See if you can find the way he went — but for goodness sake, don't run into any danger.

N.B.: Knitting needles make handy pointers, but if you are at all nervous you may take a paper-knife.

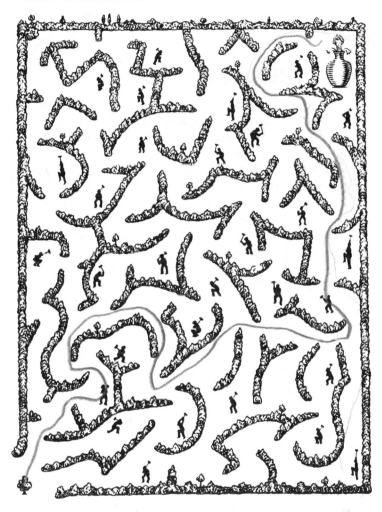

No. 6

Medium

No. 7
FINDING THE CLUE

An English prisoner had once escaped from the old fortress of Casava by picking a number of locks, and this so enraged Don Miguel Montojo that he built a new castle in the form of a maze. When he threw Sir Roger de Cleverly into the central dungeon, he defied him to escape even though there was not a single door in the whole place.

As a matter of fact there were no less than twelve ways out, but Sir Roger was unable to discover this useful fact without a plan. Nevertheless, on one of his futile wanderings he passed near a guard-room where he overheard a conversation. One of the guards was explaining to a novice the clue to the surest — though not the shortest — way of escape, and Sir Roger lost no time in putting his information to practical use.

What was the clue?

Hint: Make notes of the turnings —"Left, left, right, left," etc., till you spot a system.

No. 7

Difficult

No. 8

A FLY HUNT

This maze is in the form of a game for two. One of you must be the Spider and the other the Fly, and you start by holding a match each at the point of your respective arrows. You move by turns, the Fly travelling only over the dotted lines, and the Spider only over the continuous ones. You may move as far as you like provided you stop whenever you come to a dew-drop, but you will find you often have a choice of ways and may dodge some dew-drops by zig-zagging round them.

The object of the Fly is to escape from the web at the small arrow at the top left-hand corner, and the object of the Spider is to catch him before he gets there. When Spider and Fly meet at the same dew-drop, the Fly is considered caught. To prevent the Spider from dodging to and fro across the Fly's exit-path, a rule must be made that neither Spider nor Fly may return to the same dew-drop without visiting at least two others in between, except for the purpose of backing out of a cul-de-sac.

The Fly starts. Who will win?

N.B.: Use safety *matches.   Otherwise, when the Spider really starts moving . . . !*

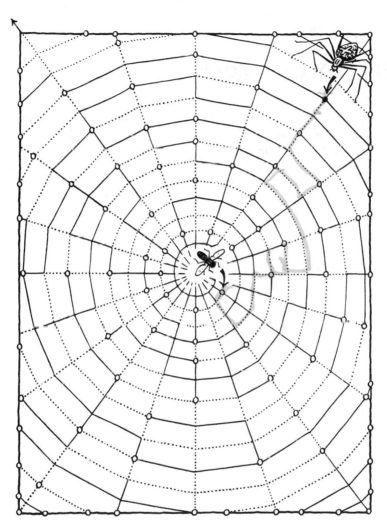

No. 8

Easy

No. 9
THE ROLLING ROAD

This puzzle being one over the eight, you are pardoned a certain amount of staggering as you make your way along the line from the arrow at the top of the diagram to the Paradise you crave. But you must pass through all the towns once and once only, and you may not pass along the same road twice.

There is only one possible way in which this can be done. What is it?

Note: The places are indicated by the dots, and unless you pass through these you do not pass through the seven places. This is a "line maze"—you run over the lines, not between them. So the pencil fiend is foiled again — or very nearly.

No. 9

Medium

No. 10
HIAWATHA'S SOUP

1. Hiram and Henrietta went visiting friends in camp, and their directions were to pass a signpost, a hostel, a windmill, an inn, a cottage and a well, and so come to the camp. Unfortunately there was no mention of the order in which these items should be taken. They found the signpost all right, but how did they proceed from there?

2. Having at last got to the camp they were disappointed to hear that there was no room for them to stay the night, and that they would have to put up at the hostel. However, they were comforted with a bowl of special soup made from the recipe of Hiawatha's deceased brother-in-law's great grandfather, sometime mayor of Medicine Hat. Now, this soup was heap big magic, and hardly had they put down their bowls than they found themselves back at the signpost again! They started off at once for the hostel, but the magic was still working and this time they arrived at their destination without having passed *any* of the other items on the way. How did they go?

Note: By all means use Hiram's stick — it has already been over the route once and should prove a reliable guide.

No. 10

Medium

No. 11
THE PROFESSOR'S JOURNEY

"Bitchester is an absolute dog's-hole for getting about in," complained Professor Bantletwog. "I had to meet my mummy at the station — special loan from Cairo, you know — and get it back to the Museum in Park Road before they locked up for the night. Here's a map of the place — see if you can find the shortest way to walk. There's a round white dot at the Museum entrance, and another one at the station, and I made the journey in twenty-five minutes, doing a good four miles per hour. I found a shorter way than the taxi driver who brought me back, but that's not surprising as it actually looks a good deal longer. See if you can spot it."

Note: The answer is given as a list of street names, and the cabman's route is also given.

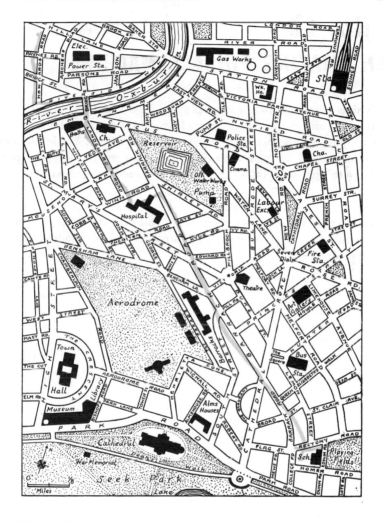

No. 11

Medium

No. 12

AN AMAZING PINBALL MACHINE

This is a game for two or more players. Take it in turns to start at the arrow and aim at the highest score. If you drop down a "hole," you at once come up another hole bearing the same letter, but in different type (case), and carry on from there. You may not retrace your path, and your turn goes on until you have scored — or have been sent back to the arrow.

Example: If you go down the small *b* you may come up at either of the capital *B*'s; if you go down the capital *A* you may come up at the small *a*, and so on.

N.B.: The obvious weapons to use in this game are pins — ordinary, hair, tie, panel, hat or belaying, but hardly safety or cotter.

No. 12

Easy

No. 13
A RESERVATION WITH RESERVATIONS

Hotel Magnifique is in difficulties. The elevators are out of action and the stairs have been freshly painted. Fortunately all the rooms are connected by doors, so the embarrassed guests are required to make their way to their apartments passing through as few occupied rooms as possible. Occupants may protect themselves by closing their doors (though some are none too particular), and visitors are told they may pass through open doors only. Your room is No. 7: how will you get to it?

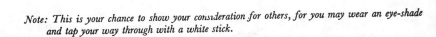

Note: This is your chance to show your consideration for others, for you may wear an eye-shade and tap your way through with a white stick.

No. 13

Easy

No. 14
CATCHING THE BOAT

Mr. Johnson — strange as it may seem — lived in a house called "H."
He had ten minutes in which to catch a boat at the Pier, "P," and his
car was waiting at the door. He had first to drive to the railway
Terminus, "T," his road taking him over or under a bridge or two, and
then to find the right platform and go by train. Can you follow his
route in the prescribed ten minutes, remembering that every wrong
turning had to be carefully retraced before he could proceed on his
way?

Reminder: Don't dig round with a pencil. Use a match.

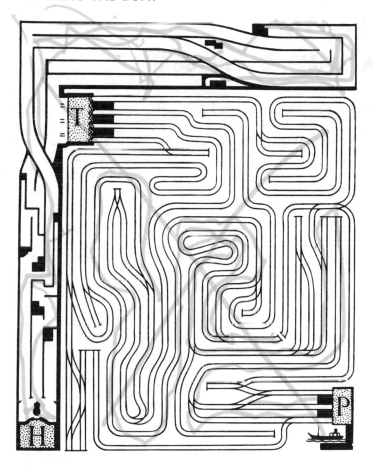

No. 14

Easy

No. 15
AN AMAZING TOBOGGAN

Starting at the top left-hand corner, toboggan to the chalet (*bottom right*) without using the same paths twice. Which way involves you in *all* the upsets? What is the fewest number of upsets you *need* have?

What price alpenstocks?

No. 15

Medium

No. 16
WHY DID HE GET THE SACK?

In order to answer this question you must first read the riddle. You may begin where you like, and may pass successively from square to square vertically, horizontally, or diagonally, but you may not jump a square. Just to make it harder, forty-one of the words are not wanted, but you must use all of the other forty-seven.

When you have read the riddle, you are not likely to be long in guessing the answer.

Hint: A good idea in puzzles of this sort is to fix the attention first on words with capital letters and punctuation marks, but don't forget that some of these may belong to the forty-one unwanted words.

One	morning	tip	night-porter	tried	puzzle	and	somehow
day	good	the	at	this	the	manager	did
he	as	shot	for	a	difficult	begged	not
had	a	train,	maze	wake	hotel	solve	to
a	dreamt	idea	usual	failed	to	return	it.
last	shot	that	his	by	home	the	again!
at	night	he	there	do	him,	try	manager
problem	this	would	could	thanking	this	him	gave
but	be	accident.	of	you!	course	sack.	the
he	serious	a	Instead	you	Of	see	oh
night-porter	failed.	not?	or	you	can	that's	why!

No. 16

Medium

No. 17

PUB CRAWL

Mr. Smith and his pals met at the Blue Boar to celebrate his Diamond
Divorce, and as it was a fine night they decided to visit the eight other
inns in the village before going home.

"Don't let's go over the same roads twice," said Mr. Smith, "and
let's finish up at the Pink Pig."

This proposal was carried *nem. con.*, and they completed their pub
crawl according to plan after sundry disputations about the order in
which the inns should be visited and the roads they should take.

As a matter of fact, there is only one way in which they could have
gone. What was it?

Note: Use a corkscrew.

No. 17

Medium

No. 18
FAITH, HOPE AND CHARITY

"You're all right to look at," said the Ogre, "but a bit too fat for my liking. I think I'll put you in the maze for a bit — *that*'ll thin you down. Oho, yes! *That*'ll thin you down!"

So Charity found herself in the centre of the Ogre's maze, and after she had done weeping she began to look about her, and presently saw some verses scratched in the wall with a rusty nail:

> Read thou these artful couplets right,
> Or else be left to die this night!
>
> The ponderous door will never ope
> Without the keys of Faith and Hope.
>
> Take no path twice — the Guards may see,
> And they know naught of Charity.
>
> Remember Poor Will.

"Now just fancy that!" said Charity. "It must be meant for me, because it mentions my name. I wonder what it means? I know, I'll just..."

She found the clue, secured the keys of Faith and Hope without traversing the same path twice, unlocked the door and made her escape.

What was the clue that she found?

Note: Don't leave tracks all round the maze with a pencil. Do it with a rusty nail.

No. 18

Medium

No. 19
POUNDING THE BEAT

The dotted line is the policeman's beat, and he must start and finish each patrol at the big dot in front of the Police Station. He may take the roads in any order provided he covers all of them on each patrol. He may not go over the same roads twice, though he may, of course, cross his own track at the road-junctions. In how many different (or partly different) ways is it possible for him to patrol his beat?

Note: This is a London policeman, for he is wearing a helmet. But alas! London policemen's helmets do not have spikes. Use something else.

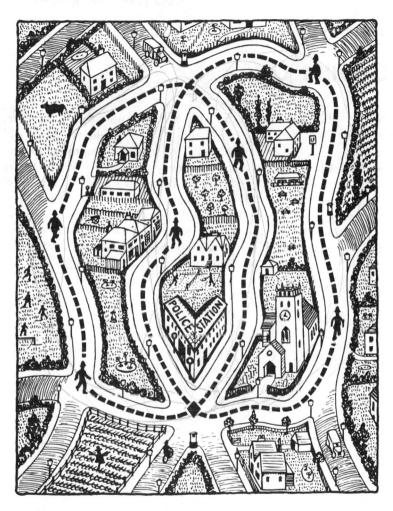

No. 19

Medium

No. 20

ALADDIN'S CAVE

After Aladdin had rubbed the lamp and been admitted to the cave, he had to pass a number of trees bearing fruits of gold and silver and precious stones. He found it impossible to resist the temptation to pick these, but of his three pockets one already contained a catapult, two marbles, some chewing gum, a smashed sparrow's egg, and a piece of string, and the others would only hold two of the precious fruits apiece. He was resolved to reserve his baggy Persian pants for the treasure in the chest at the further corner of the cave, and he was able to keep this resolution by choosing a path which took him past four trees only, from each of which he picked one fruit.

Which way did he go?

Reminder: You oughtn't to need one by this time.

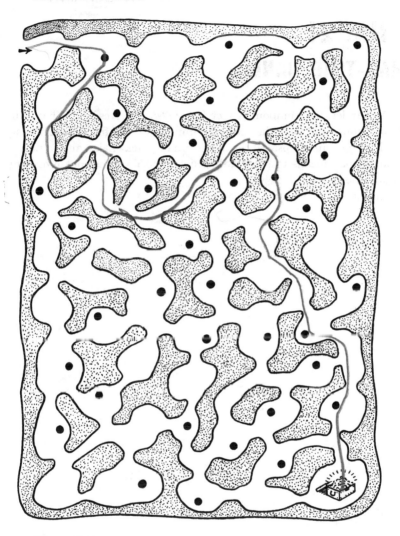

No. 20

Medium

No. 21
RAG-TIME BAND

Alexander, the trombone player (*bottom left*), arrives late. What is the fewest number of ladies he need pass immediately in front of on his way to the bandstand steps? All the ladies are in black chairs, and to pass in front of one means to cross a dotted line. (You may not cross any continuous lines.)

At a guess, how many ladies are present?

Note: Don't be silly — a trombone is much too thick! Use a baton.

No. 21

Easy

No. 22
DODGING THE MINES

This looks like an ordinary maze, but it does, in fact, involve a psychological factor which will have various effects on different readers. It was found among the papers of a naval spy, who claimed it to be a plan of the intricate mine-fields in the Straits of Dover. There is only one way of steering a ship safely through from Dover to Calais, and you should discover it in less than a quarter of an hour. But look well ahead as you solve the problem, for if you enter a blind alley you are to be considered sunk.

Reminder: Put that pencil away; use a firing-pin instead.

No. 22

Medium

No. 23

YE GAME AND PLAYE OF YE "WOKKA"

"Wokka" is a Cockney name for the game of dominoes which some call "Honest John," and it is the simplest of all the domino games. Two of you should play this adaptation of it, one starting at the double-six and the other at the double-one. You play in turns, moving as usual from six to six, three to three, two to two, and so on, and the object here is to see who can reach the double-blank in the centre first. It is possible for each player to attain this object *via* fifteen dominoes. If you get stuck, you must forfeit a turn and then you may proceed from any domino adjacent to the one you got stuck at, this being our maze equivalent to taking one out of the pool.

You may make it a simple maze for one player by finding your way right across the diagram from the double-six to the double-one, in thirty stages, the middle one of which should be the double-blank.

Note: In the proper game of "Wokka," you do not aim at playing the double-blank, but simply at getting rid of all your dominoes, of which you have seven each, and a pool of fourteen from which to draw when necessary.

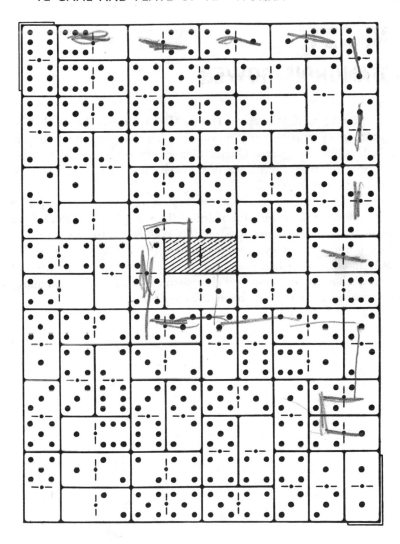

No. 23

Easy

No. 24

ROSAMUND'S BOWER

Rosamund was a Mistress of Henry II, and legend has it that he built a maze at his palace at Woodstock in which he kept her safe from the jealousy of the Queen. Queen Eleanor, however, is said to have penetrated the maze by means of a silken clue, and to have forced Rosamund to drink poison.

That was a long time ago — about 1176 A.D., it would be — yet up till the seventeenth century the ruins of the maze in Woodstock Park were shown to visitors, and Rosamund's Well is still to be seen there.

Now put on your crown, and, pretending to be Henry II, pay a visit to Rosamund. And when you have done that, try guessing (without counting) how many rooms and compartments there are in the maze, how many open doors, and how many closed doors.

Note: By the way, those knitting needles of Rosamund's ought to remind you of something.

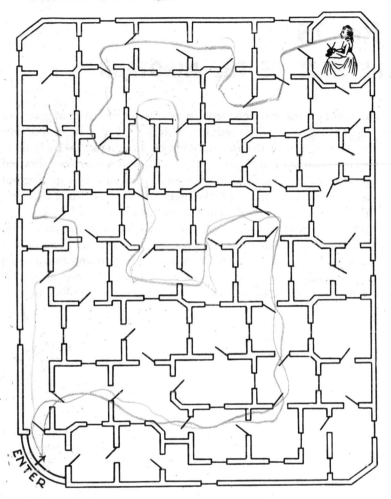

No. 24

Easy

No. 25

THE MAZE OF THE MINOTAUR

This is not the maze which Dedalus built (which is given on page viii) but the wicked maze of Tweedalus, who flourished a thousand years before the creation of the moon. Wrongly attributed to Dedalus by medieval scholars, it is probably the most ingenious maze ever devised.

Apart from the mathematical chances against your ever getting out, the designer has introduced psychological factors with such ingenuity that the effective chances of escape dwindle almost to nil.

If the passages of this maze were a yard wide, and its walls a foot thick, the only path out would be little short of a mile in length, and you would be likely to go crazy or die of exhaustion and hunger long before you found it. On the opposite page, however, you can see the complete plan of the maze and may hope to solve it within half an hour.

Note: This is where that ancient gold toothpick of great-grandfather comes in handy.

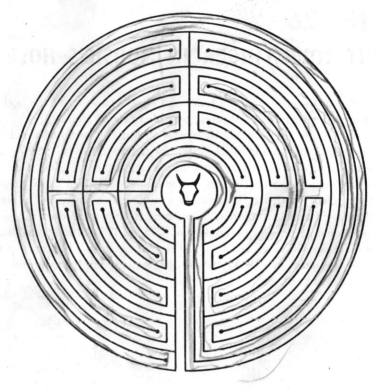

No. 25

Difficult

No. 26

PUT YOUR FINGER IN MOUSIE'S HOLE

Put your finger in mousie's hole, and mousie runs out at the bottom right-hand corner by the shortest possible route. Which is it?

You do this "solid" maze by eye. A curious, but unintentional feature of this maze was discovered after it was drawn. It is this: Supposing the mouse to be lost and to put into operation the old trick of always keeping in contact with the wall of the tunnel, he will run straight into a mouse-trap whether he keeps always to the left or always to the right. (Be it noted that this method of escaping from a maze does not work where some portions of the maze are isolated. It would get you out of the mazes shown in Figs. 8 and 9 in the introductory chapter, but not out of the maze in Fig. 11, where you would simply go round and round the isolated centre.)

Note: This is a "solid" maze, the paths running in three dimensions. They are represented in perspective, and where you can see that one path runs behind another you may follow it round. You do not stop, as you do in flat mazes, just because an ink line on the paper happens to cross your path.

No. 26

Easy

No. 27
THE TANGLED TELETAPE

The three gamblers await news of the race from the teleprinter, but which of them are looking at the right side of the tape? Starting at the machine you must follow the tape round by eye alone.

Note: No pointers allowed — and no betting, please!

No. 27

Medium

No. 28

SEASIDE HOLIDAY

Eight families, living in eight London suburbs, all decide to go to the sea for a holiday at the same time. The railway connections forbid them to travel through each other's suburbs, or through London itself, and they are obliged to stop at the first town they come to. For convenience, dots marking the ends of all journeys have been placed at the towns, while the suburbs themselves have been numbered. The families from Nos. 1, 2, 3, and 4 arrange to spend their holidays at the same place, and so do the families from Nos. 5, 6, 7, and 8. But the second group of families, being snobs, decide to go to a place to which the first group cannot go. Find the two places.

Note: This is not a difficult problem, though it is likely to take some time. It is really eight easy puzzles on the same diagram, followed by an examination of the solutions.

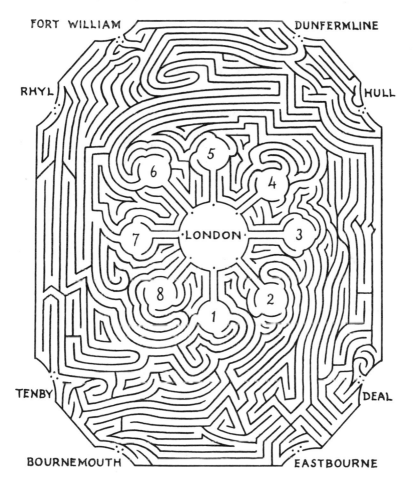

No. 28

Medium

No. 29

THE TABLET OF FUM HOAM

The traveller Lemuel Polo was rummaging among the ruins of the ancient city of Yo-Yo when he discovered a thin clay tablet scored with a series of concentric spirals, one of which led the curious eye to the Chinese character for the "Eternal" in the centre. He knew that this must be the famous Tablet of Fum Hoam, the great philosopher of the Ping Dynasty, and he decided to bring it home to the British Museum. In picking it up, however, he broke it into five large pieces and a number of fragments too small to retrieve, and hastened to embed the large pieces in pitch before he forgot their relative places.

On the journey home his ship passed through the tropics, where the heat of the sun softened the pitch and all the pieces became displaced by half a turn of their spiral markings. Some had slipped inwards half a turn, and some outwards, and the only way to discover what had happened was to trace out the main spiral, the beginning of which Lemuel Polo had been careful to mark on the pitch with an arrow.

It is quite easy to arrive at the centre by pursuing an arbitrary course, but that will not solve the problem. At each fracture the solver has a choice of two ways only, but to follow the correct path he must always make the same choice whenever he crosses the same fracture. The problem has been rendered easier by the presence of a few cracks which happen to bar the way to some wrong paths, and thus there is only one possible answer to the problem which is — in what manner were the four pieces, A, B, C, D, displaced?

Hint: The answer given assumes that one or other of the pieces (it does not matter which) stands correct with regard to the centre. The movements of the others are then compared with this standard.

No. 29

Difficult

No. 30
THE CASTLE MAZE

The King was in his Counting House,
 Counting out his money;
The pile of household bills, he swore,
 Was anything but funny.

"My books won't balance," he complained,
 "I'll with the Queen confer,"
And he rang up sixpence-halfpenny on
 The gold cash-register.

He grabbed the bills and started off
 To seek his thriftless Queen.
"When these are paid," he moaned, "we simp-
 ly shall not have a bean!

"I've missed the way, I do declare!
 I'm lost in my own house!
*Can no kind friend show me the way
 To reach my Royal Spouse?*"

Alas! he wandered round and round,
 Caught in the Castle Maze,
And they only found his body
 After twenty-seven days.

And all that time the Queen stayed up,
 Waiting to go to bed.
"He always comes and kisses me,
 And says good-night!" she said.

Yes — the Queen was in her Parlour,
 Eating bread and honey . . .
At last she bust, but no one knows
 What happened to the money.

*N.B.: Creditors should apply at the County Court, Tradesmen's Entrance. It is unnecessary
to bring a pencil; use your wits instead (there's a catch in it).*

No. 30

Easy

No. 31
TREASURE ISLAND

Gangster Gus, of Gunnersbury (which is so-called because — but never mind that now), buried his treasure in the south-west corner of the island shown in the chart opposite. He lived at The Haven, a village whose chief industries are fishing and golf-ball renovating, and which is situated on the harbour at the north-east. Whenever Gangster Gus had treasure to stow away he used to drive to his *cache* on a moonless night and return in time for breakfast. Thus his wife, who knew her Gus backwards and called him "Sug" in consequence, never, never wondered where he had been. But in order to do this, Gus was obliged to travel by the shortest route, and the problem is to decide which, of all the possible routes, this was, and to do it by inspection of the map without measuring-instruments.

Note: The answer is given as a list of the places passed through.

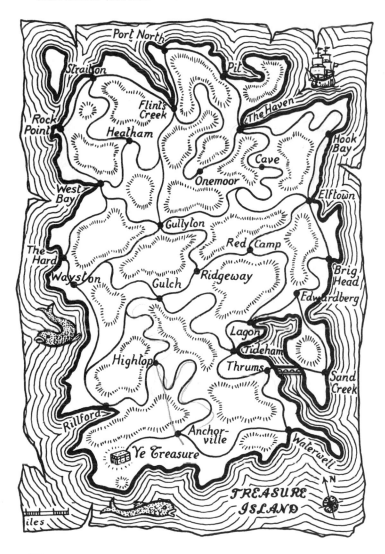

No. 31

Medium

No. 32
THE KNIGHT'S TALE

There is no doubt that Sir Jingo Yarn, Kt., was a liar, for when asked by the police if he knew how his uncle had died, he told the tale given on the opposite page. After duly considering this, the Inspector decided to use it in evidence against him, and your task is first of all to read it and then to discover how the Inspector knew it was a falsehood.

Note: Unlike Problem No. 16 there are no superfluous words in this puzzle.

in-stantly."	"I	club	The	w...	how	brains	among
to	him.	effect	know	his	worst	he	morning,
the	died	about	after	he	Sunday	them,	out
was	The	sermon	"He	creditors	man	and	if
he	during	were	died	last	Yarn.	when	s
pulpit	fear,	was	Jingo	he	his	he	dreamt
asleep	clubbed;	cause	thumped	said	really	had	the
to	the	Sir	been	real	parson	that	had

No. 32

Difficult

morning and dreamt that his creditors were after him!

I know how he died said Sir Jingo Yarn. He was asleep during the sermon last Sunday when the Parson thumped the pulpit. The effect was as if he had really been clubbed; he died instantly."

The worst among them, a man he had real cause to fear was about to club his brains out

No. 33
THE CASTLE TELEPHONES

When the eccentric Viscount Suspectem decided to have an internal telephone system installed in his castle, he insisted that the five lines from the Hall to the Morning Room, Study, Octagonal Tower, Telephone Box, and Cellars, should be kept separate so that conversations could not be accidentally overheard. The lines were to run from A to A′, B to B′, C to C′, D to D′, and E to E′, but they were never to cross one another or to pass through the same rooms or corridors.

This was a stiff problem, and the engineers finally wrote down the letters in their approximate positions on a blank sheet of paper, and after connecting them up with lines which never crossed, transferred them to the plan, fitting them into the rooms and corridors so that each had a separate path of its own. There is only one way in which this could have been done. What was it?

Advice: Don't do your rough work on too small a sheet of paper. It is twice as easy when drawn on a large scale.

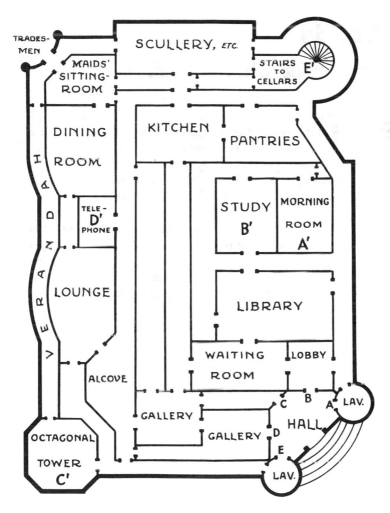

No. 33

Difficult

No. 34

GENTLEMEN OF THE ROAD

1. Start with the cyclists (*top right*) and go to the Dew Drop for tea. What is the smallest number of tramps you need pass?

2. After tea, starting at the Dew Drop, pay a visit to *all* the tramps in turn without going over the same roads twice, and return to the Dew Drop for a beer.

Note: Take a spoke out of your wheel — anything rather than make pencil marks all over these nice country lanes.

No. 34

Medium

No. 35

THE PLUMBER'S PROBLEM

Mr. Fawcet was a jobbing plumber, and he had been told to examine a tank full of pipes which some apprentices had been joining together for practice. His instructions were to remove all unnecessary piping, leaving only the shortest way through for a flow of water.

Which pipes did he leave?

Note: This is a "solid" maze again, and the note at the foot of No. 26 explains this type of puzzle.

Reminder: You won't do any good digging round with a pencil, but if you must use one, forbear to make any marks till you have thoroughly examined the tangle of pipes by eye. And then let your marks be faint ones — remember Mr. Fawcet had to do without a pencil at all.

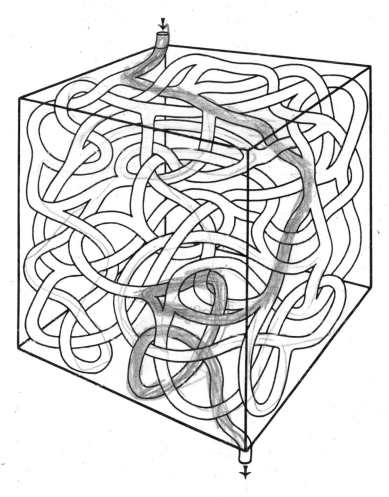

No. 35

Medium

No. 36

SHOPPING DAY IN NEW YORK CITY

"Now, Billy, get out of the car and run and do Mamma's shopping for her."

"What's this list for, Mamma?"

"Ssh! That's your shopping list, Billy. There are 86 shops to go to, and I don't want you to waste any time. Remember Mamma's waiting. You mustn't pass any shop twice, no matter which side of the road you are on, and at your 11th corner you can buy yourself a bag of popcorn. That'll be — let me see — your 47th shop, and as it's by the Monument at the end of the road you can wave to me. Now, off you go — here's a bag of gold.

"Oh, and Billy! Your tour will be done in 23 straight lines, not that that matters in the least, but you're not to go through the Park and you'll turn 22 corners all told and don't you dare go into the School or have a Public Bath and don't forget to wave to me from the candy-shop and *do* hurry up because Mamma's waiting."

"O.K. I'm off! . . . Say, you guys — can you tell me which way I gotta go?"

Note: This is another puzzle in which tracing paper would be useful.

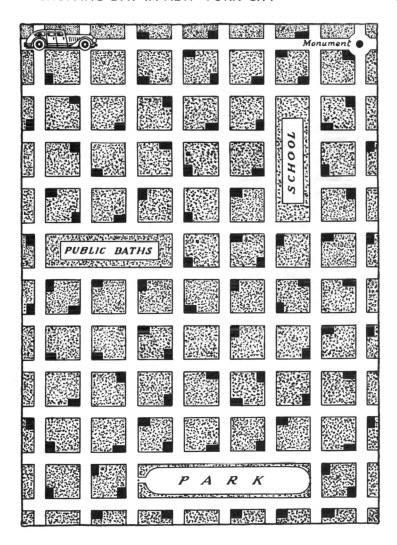

Monument

SCHOOL

PUBLIC BATHS

PARK

No. 36

Difficult

No. 37

PORTRAIT OF THE ARTIST AS A YOUNG MAN

Admirers of Surrealism (or perhaps Anti-art) will understand this at once. "What a striking likeness!" they will exclaim. "See how he walks with his eye always on the ground, his head full of illusions and elementary mathematics! Marvellous! If we met him in the street we should know him instantly."

The problem for the ordinary reader, however, is not to recognise the artist but to unravel his illusions, and this must be done by eye only. Pick up the thread at the arrow marked "O," and follow it through all the obstacles till you arrive at one of the numbers along the top of the picture.

Note: Although a pointer is not to be used, astigmatic readers may be pardoned for infringing this regulation as regards the large spiral figures at the bottom.

No. 37

Medium

No. 38

EXTRA RUMMY

This is another game for two, one starting at the ace of Hearts and the other at the ace of Diamonds. The object is to reach the ace of Spades in the centre, but the players may only move so as to make a run of three (or more), a flush of three (or more), or a pair. If a player finds himself unable to proceed further, he must use his next few turns returning to a point where he has a choice of routes to follow.

A player may use either one or two cards of his last "show" to assist in making up his next. Thus, he may make a run of 4, 5, 6, and at his next move he may make a flush of the 5, 6 and another card, if they are all of the same suit. The *last* card in each turn will always, of course, be part of the next turn — generally the first card of it.

Example starting at the ace of Hearts: A player could go 1, 2, 3, for his first move, which takes him to the 3 of Spades. For his next move he could go to the 6 of Spades, because this makes a flush with the 2 and 3. His third move could take him to the 6 of Hearts (a pair), and then he could return to the ace of Hearts again by means of the flush.

It is possible for each player to reach the ace of Spades *via* 27 cards. The diagram may also be used as a sort of "Patience" game for one, by working right across the diagram from the ace of Hearts to the ace of Diamonds, taking in the ace of Spades on the way.

Note: Runs must be made in numerical order — 1, 2, 3, etc. — and must not run backwards.
Flushes must be all of the same suit.

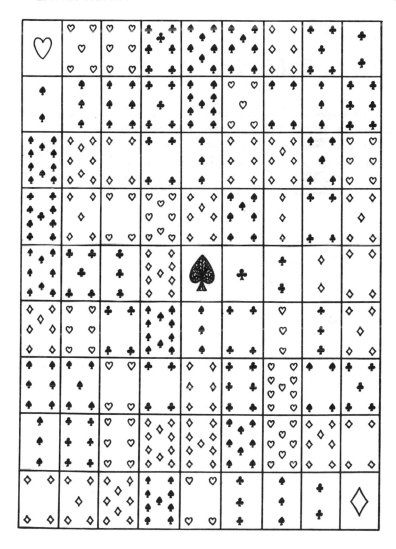

No. 38

Medium

No. 39
GETTING THROUGH THE WIRE

Private Higgs and Private Hoggs were told to find a way through a barbed-wire entanglement, and they were given a pair of wire-cutters to assist them. The (alternate) posts on their side of the entanglement are numbered 1, 2, 3, . . . , 6, and they had to make their way to the posts lettered A, B, C, . . . , F, but their wire-cutters were so blunt that they could only make five cuts. They managed the job without getting up to any tricks, but how did they do it?

Reminder: Use a pin instead.

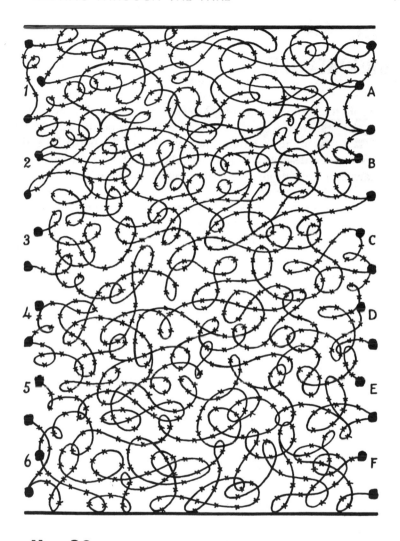

No. 39

Medium

No. 40
HORRORSCOPE

"Astrobottle," the famous astrologer, was once careless enough to confuse his star-map with the label on a brandy bottle, and he was found late that night examining the sky through the bottle instead of his telescope. Bottle-glass does not make the best of telescope lenses, and the stars appeared to go round and round the Pole Star with such velocity that Astrobottle felt quite giddy. To steady himself, he traced a path among their fiery tracks to the central Pole Star, beginning at the moon which was then on the horizon.

See if you can do the same.

N.B.: This is another occasion on which a corkscrew would seem to be the appropriate pointer to use.

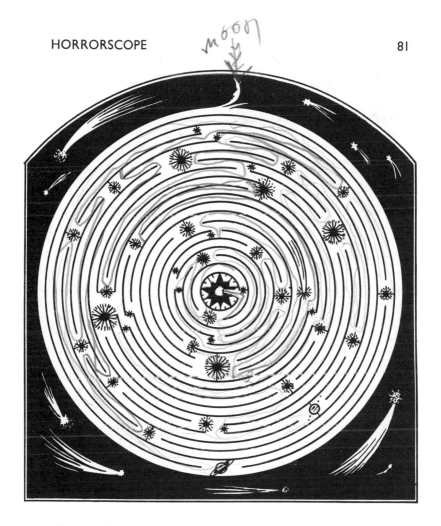

No. 40

Medium

No. 41
THE ANSWER'S A — !

There was a shortage of lemons in the town of Dripton-on-Slop, but it got about that Sir Patrick O'Crazy had been hoarding them and had hidden one of incredible size in his garden maze. Now the Dripton Dribblers were due to play the Bugville Bargers in the local cup-tie soccer match, and their captain was determined they shouldn't lose for want of a lemon to pass round at half-time. He therefore penetrated Sir Patrick's maze and secured the prize fruit in spite of repeated blows from the gardener's mallets. Each blow knocked him out for five minutes, yet he reached the lemon having spent only twenty minutes in an unconscious condition.

Begin at the bottom left-hand corner, and see if you can find the way the Dripton captain must have taken.

Note: There is a certain peculiarity about this maze, when compared with another maze in this book. To which other maze do we refer, and what is the peculiarity?

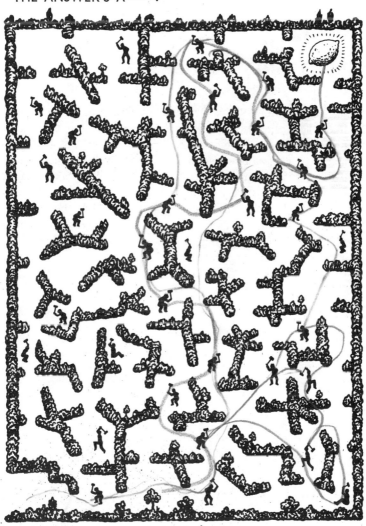

No. 41

Medium

No. 42
"SNAKES AND LADDERS"

"Snakes and Ladders" is a very ancient game, and something very much like it was played by the Babylonians in the year B.C. Here we present a maze based on the game, and the problem is to get from the circle marked "1" (*top left-hand corner*) to the circle marked "2" (*top right-hand corner*). You may only go *down* the snakes, and *up* the ladders, though it is to be pointed out that going "down the snakes" means being swallowed by them, and sometimes takes you *up* the page.

You must move from circle to circle, and these have been irregularly numbered to facilitate recording the answer. The journey from "1" to "2" can be made in sixteen moves.

Reminder: By all means use a serpent's fang or the rung of a ladder, but don't scribble all over the maze with your pencil — which should be reserved for jotting down the numbers. The best way to thread this maze is by eye alone.

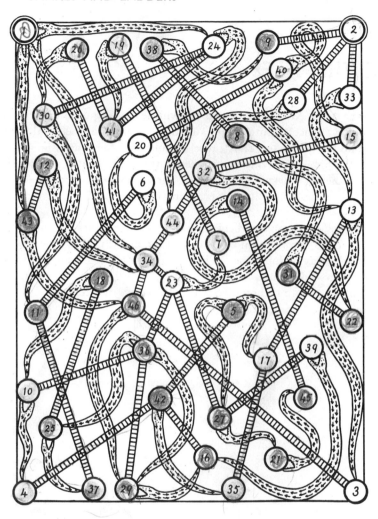

No. 42

Medium

1,43,46,29,16,42,5,27,21,45,19,22,

31,8,38,9,2

No. 43
ON THE TILES

Charwoman Neligan Millicent Entwhistle was required to scrub the tiles in the chancel of Bitchester Cathedral, and so that she shouldn't do the same tile twice and thus cause trouble with her trades union, she was in the habit of leaving her bucket on the tile indicated and starting work on the tile marked by the brush. She then worked from one to the other in a series of straight lines, going over each tile once and once only.

At first she accomplished this task in 37 straight lines, because three of them made her initial in the centre of the diagram, but after a while she found a way of doing the job in only 23 straight lines, some of which were of course, diagonal.

See if you can find these two ways of covering the tiles.

Note: Since there are two solutions to be found, this is a puzzle in which some sort of tracing paper would be useful. Alternatively, the problem is simple enough to transfer to squared paper, or to copy.

No. 43

Difficult

No. 44
KITTEN'S KNITTING

Popsy, the kitten, having tangled up five skeins of differently coloured wool, Popsy, the pickaninny, had to disentangle them. One end of each of the skeins is indicated at the top of the diagram, and the other ends are numbered along the bottom. The problem is to discover the colours of the numbered ends.

See if you can trace the threads with your unaided eye.

Note: This is strictly an "eye" maze, but a knitting-needle may be used as a last resort.

RED YELLOW GREEN BROWN BLUE

2   3   4   5

No. 44

Easy

No. 45
FUN WITH FUNGI

Start at the basket and see if you can get to the mushroom, but beware of picking the toadstool by mistake! The rule of the road is that you may not go against the small arrows or traverse the same road twice.

Note: Borrow the arrow off the top of the basket — you won't need it again.

No. 45

Medium

No. 46
ARCHIE THE ALCHEMIST

Yes! Archie the Alchemist has discovered how to make Gold from Lead, Iron, Brass, and Tin. If he starts with Lead, in what order must he take the other three ingredients so as to finish with Gold? (You must include all the metals in your process, and you may not travel the same tubes twice, nor cross a line.)

Note: A broomstick would seem to be appropriate, wouldn' t it?

No. 46

Easy

Lead
tin gold
Iron

No. 47

THE SHUNTER'S PROBLEM

Bill Buffer, the world-famous shunter, had a train of thirty-nine freight cars at X. His job was to get as many of these as possible to Y, but every time he backed out of a siding he left one car behind. He shunted his cars from X to Y losing only nineteen on the way.

How did he do it?

Note: The numbers on the diagram are merely to enable a clear solution to be given.

Reminder: No, you remind us this time.

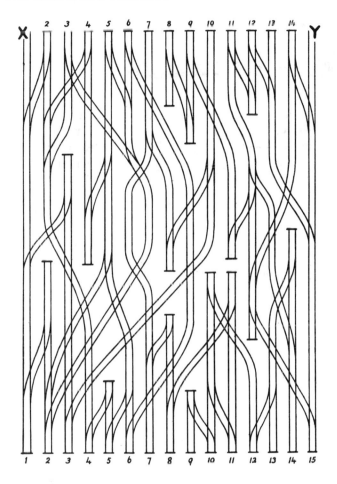

No. 47

Medium

No. 48
THE PHILADELPHIA MAZE

This famous maze is something of a curiosity. It is somewhat dazzling to look at for long, and that may perhaps account for the fact that about the year 1903 it drove a Philadelphia businessman crazy. The problem is to find how many different ways there are of getting to the centre, and the gentleman of Philadelphia mentioned above shot himself in despair before reaching the solution.

The reader is warned that the answer is far in excess of a hundred, and that the problem must therefore be tackled by a more systematic method than that of trial and error — unless it is desired to spend several years on it!

The method to use is that explained in the solution to Problem No. 19, which was, however, a much more simple puzzle.

Warning: Pencil lines on this *maze will only make confusion worse confounded.*

No. 48

Difficult

No. 49
THE SPIDER AND THE FLY

"Won't you walk into my parlour?"
    Said the Spider to the Fly.
"No, thank you!" said the other, "Not
    Unless you tell me why.

"The fact is, all my feet are stuck,
    And I've a sort of hunch
That I must struggle free again
    Or figure in your lunch!"

"How right you are!" the Spider said,
    "But sure as I'm a sinner,
I've got five minutes' tight-rope walk
    Before I catch my dinner!"

"Why, that's O.K!" the Fly declared,
    "I'll only be a minute!
By all means try to catch your lunch
    But you will never win it!"

Note: Starting at the Spider's fore-legs, see if you can catch the Fly in less than one minute, travelling over the continuous lines only.

No. 49

Easy

No. 50
PIPS TO YOU!

Here are twelve puzzles in one. Choose any two of the card pips and, entering the maze by one of them, aim to get out by the other. Six combinations are possible, and you can do them all (*a*) passing the door of the summer-house, or (*b*) without passing the door of the summer-house. You may not go over the same paths twice in any single turn.

N.B.: Quite a lot of tracing-paper would be handy.

No. 50

Medium

HOW TO AMAZE YOUR FRIENDS

THERE is just as much enjoyment to be had in devising mazes as in threading them, and since most kinds are best designed on squared paper, no brilliant gift of drawing is necessary. A page from a school arithmetic exercise-book is excellent for the purpose, or a sheet of paper may be ruled faintly into quarter-inch squares. A serviceable size is 20 quarter-inches by 30, and you construct your maze by going more heavily over the lines you intend to show. Afterwards, you ink these in and rub out all the rest if they annoy you. Examples in this book of mazes made in precisely this fashion are Nos. 7, 18, 22 and 28, and also the less orthodox mazes, 1, 4 ,14 and 36.

Mazes with curves generally have to be done freehand, but Nos. 25, 40 and 48 consist of concentric circles done with a pair of compasses, while even the spirals of Nos. 5 and 29 began as compass-drawn circles and were afterwards adapted by freehand. Irregular curves demand some artistic ability, for it is not unimportant that a maze should please the eye as well as tantalize the mind. When an irregular maze has been drawn, it is often advisable to mould it into a more or less harmonious pattern by lengthening a curve here, sharpening an angle there, and so on. The reader would probably be surprised at the amount of time spent on this part of the job in such mazes as Nos. 9, 15 and 26. Even in straight-line mazes it is as well not to have too many vertical or horizontal paths crowded together, and to distribute the occasions of choice with judiciousness and circumspection.

With almost any sort of maze it is profitable to begin by roughly marking in the solution. This may have to be modified as the work proceeds, as curious little snags sometimes turn up in the form of mechanical difficulties. For instance, when five quarter-inch pathways demand to go through a space only one inch wide, some drastic alteration may be necessary if none of them can be otherwise diverted. But this is part of the fun of maze-making; such difficulties are the counterparts of those which the maze-threader enjoys when he solves your completed puzzle.

Mazes involving a problem other than finding a path to a goal are best drawn roughly in simplified form first. The reader may be interested in the original rough sketch for No. 17, by way of example, and we have therefore rescued this from the waste paper basket to provide Fig. 13. With this crude plan before us we placed the inns in a more or less balanced arrangement on a fresh sheet of paper, and simply complicated the paths between them without departing from the conditions which prevent alternative solutions. ("No way" meant that no

way was to be provided without involving travelling over the same
paths twice).

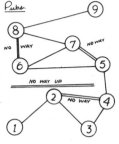

FIG. 13

Supposing the solution of a maze to be decided upon and to be
roughly marked in, there are a number of legitimate tricks to be made
use of in filling up the rest of the diagram. These are all, by the nature
of the subject, psychological devices; purely mechanical tricks, such as
making some of the essential gaps so small that the solver will either
overlook them or put them down to accidents in drawing or printing,
are dishonest — and, what is possibly worse, mean. The utmost that
may be allowed are such devices as that illustrated in the solution to
No. 30, which may appeal to the wit or sense of humour of the solver.
At all costs, the drawing must be *mechanically* honest and clear, and, by
the same token, the statement of any additional problem involved must
give all vital factors without *grammatical* obscurity. Such statements
may, of course, be given cryptically provided the reader is given a fair
hint that they are cryptic — perhaps by breaking into rhyme or tongue-
twisting, or by being too outrageous to be taken literally. Never assume
special knowledge in the reader, but such general knowledge as that
required for the solution of No. 9 may be allowed as long as the problem
is capable of solution without it. (No. 32 is a different case, since it is
an example of a well-known type of problem whose nature is hinted at
in the title).

The chief legitimate tricks are as follows :

First, however good a solver's intentions may be, he will sooner or
later be tempted to start the maze from the wrong end. Therefore,
always run at least one "blind" backwards from the goal. This must,
of course, be made sufficiently complex to keep him hesitating, yet it
must not occupy too much space as it is merely a subsidiary item.

Second, most people are right-handed and in any given number of
choices they will turn to the right more often than they will to the left.
Therefore, more than half the turns in your solution should be left-
hand ones, and your most ingenious blinds should run off the true path
by conspicuous right-hand turnings.

Third, do not hesitate to make use of the time-honoured catch of running false paths steadily inwards towards the centre, while the true path migrates to the outer edge of the maze and actually runs some distance in the *wrong* direction before making a surprise turn to the goal. When the true path does run towards the goal, let two or more false paths run parallel with it for some distance. Then the threader of the maze, learning by experience of the false paths that that way leads nowhere, may be persuaded to neglect the true path also. This principle was reduced to a system in the preparation of No. 22. A maze with very wide passages was first completed, and then a line was ruled down the centre of each pathway, thus virtually doubling the size of the maze by providing a complete set of false passages parallel with all existing ones.

Fourth, by all means let some of your blinds run into each other, after sufficient winding, but make sure they do not provide a short-cut to the goal. It is as well to connect together only those passages which leave the correct path at points near one another, for when the threader comes back from a detour almost to the very place from which he started, he will not be inclined to dispute which is the better path! By all means connect together the various tributaries which run off from the *same* blind passage; indeed, systems subsidiary to the blind passages are what make the maze difficult enough to warrant infliction on friends and enemies, and they may be as complex as you please.

Fifth, avoid concentrating a group of blind passages into a small area, for the eye can often take in such a group as a whole and see at a glance that it is circumscribed by an unbroken line. No part of the maze must thus betray its nature, but when it seems unavoidable to prevent such simplicity, the mind of the maze-threader may sometimes be frustrated by the devices described in the following paragraph.

Sixth, purely psychological obstacles may be provided in a number of ways. The suggestion of irrelevant objects by the shapes outlined by the passages is one. For instance, the mere sight of such patterns as those in Nos. 5, 17, 26 and 35 cause the subconscious mind to echo Kipp's awed whisper, "Choobs!" The maze-threader is fascinated — he knows not why — by such intestinal displays, and he may be dazed sufficiently to prevent his grasping on sight the futility of exploring certain groups of blind passages. Sprawling limbs, contorted bodies, staring eyes, and even phallic symbols, may be used, but they must be so drawn as to awaken recognition in the subconscious mind without being openly perceived. To give an example, a small circle or almond-shape, emphasized by careful placing or suitable thickening of lines, is effectively symbolical of the compelling eye.

Seventh, the eye itself may be played upon in certain kinds of maze.

We include one — No. 37 — which depends entirely upon optical illusions for its difficulty, but Fig. 14 illustrates another sort of visual

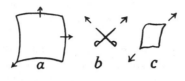

FIG. 14

trap which may sometimes be used. The distorted square is taken from No. 4, and its effect depends on the fact that the eye chooses rather to leave the square by the convexities and points, indicated by the arrows at *a*, than to brave the concavities. It also prefers to follow the points of the scissors and the sharp angles of the "paper," as shown at *b* and *c*, respectively. Needless to say, the maze is so designed that if the eye succumbs to this natural impulse it will never solve the problem.

The reader may feel that we have over-burdened this subject of maze-devising with unnecessary rules and principles; that all this big talk of "psychology" and "illusion" and "legitimate devices," and so forth, is pretentious for so trivial a subject. He may even have begun to doubt if it is worth while coping with these problems himself, and be tempted to accuse us of giving a false idea of the simplicity of maze-making at the beginning of this chapter.

If he feels that way about it, we would hasten to point out that the list of legitimate tricks-of-the-trade given in the foregoing paragraphs is merely by way of refinement on an essentially simple idea, and emerged from an *analysis* of successful mazes drawn to no established rule or principle at all. In short, if the subject of mazes does appeal to the reader, his own native instinct and cunning will lead him unawares along the paths indicated, and the points here elaborated are chiefly an attempt to provide some sort of understanding of the effectiveness of mazes. They are not so much a set of instructions as an explanation of the magic.

Draw your maze first. If it is successful in amusing and amazing your friends, you may find pleasure in analysing it yourself. If it does not attract them — why, then it is hoped that consideration of the above points may help you to improve by art what nature has for once failed to accomplish. The subject of mazes *can* be both interesting and fascinating — much depends, as we said in our introductory chapter, on the mood you happen to be in at the moment.

SOLUTIONS

No. 1 THE HALL OF SEVENTY ROOMS

After entering the Hall, Abou Ben 'Ad 'Em kept his left hand in contact with the wall as he wandered round the rooms. By the time he reached his first room in the third row from the top his left arm began to ache, so he changed over to the right-hand wall, and, hugging that, arrived at the Treasure-Chamber without difficulty.

No. 2 A TANGLED TALE

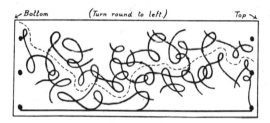

No. 3 THE GOLDEN APPLE

Start up the main left-hand trunk, cross to the right-hand trunk, and soon after cross back again. Then keep to your right till you are once more on the right-hand half of the picture, and the rest is easily found by trial and error.

No. 4 SCISSORS CUT PAPER

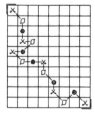

The diagram contains 25 pairs of scissors, 24 pieces of paper, and 31 stones.

No. 5 CATCHING THE ADDER

The correct tail is the bottom left-hand one, and the solution may be found by trial and error.

No. 6　ALLEY BARBER AND THE THIRTY THUGS

No. 7　FINDING THE CLUE

The clue was to take two left-hand turnings in succession, and then one right-hand turning, repeating the procedure till the right-hand door in the top wall was reached. The turnings are counted only where there is a choice of ways.

No. 9　THE ROLLING ROAD

This puzzle is not difficult provided you take the towns in their right order, and that is given in G. K. Chesterton's famous poem, "Before the Roman Came to Rye," as follows: Beachy Head, Birmingham, Goodwin Sands, Glastonbury, Brighton Pier, Bannockburn, Kensal Green, Paradise.

No. 10　HIAWATHA'S SOUP

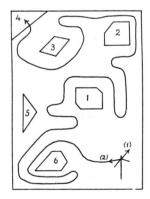

1. Starting in the direction indicated on the signpost, Hiram and Henrietta passed the items in the order in which they are numbered.
2. The diagram shows their second journey, slightly simplified.

No. 11   THE PROFESSOR'S JOURNEY

The quickest — i.e., shortest — way is: High Street, Mousehole Lane, Flint Road, Yeo Avenue, Barrack Road, Circus Road, Amy Lane, Woodburn Terrace, Station Road. A taxi driver would probably have started off along Park Road, Cathedral Road, Seven Dials, and then taken either New Road and North Street or continued up Cathedral Road to Chapel Street and Terminus Road. You may check these routes with a map-measurer or a piece of cotton.

No. 13   A RESERVATION WITH RESERVATIONS

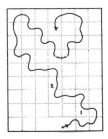

No. 14   CATCHING THE BOAT

Mr. Johnson takes the left-hand road from his house and goes *over* the first bridge. He turns right at the top of the diagram, and takes the first on the right into what looks like a yard. Passing *under* the second bridge (from right to left), and following the road *under* the first bridge, he then backs up to the station. His platform is the second one from the top, and thereafter the engine-driver manages without much difficulty. He does, however, have to enter one or two sidings and back out of them along different lines. He eventually pulls up in the top platform of the Pier station.

No. 15   AN AMAZING TOBOGGAN

In this simplified diagram you follow the lines (not the spaces between the lines, as in the puzzle). The continuous line shows your general direction when you suffer *all* the upsets; the broken line, how you need have only *one* upset.

No. 16 WHY DID HE GET THE SACK ?

"One morning the night-porter at a hotel begged the manager not to return home by his usual train, as he had dreamt last night that there would be a serious accident. Instead of thanking him, the manager gave him the sack. Of course you can see why!" And the answer to *that* is that the night-porter had no business to be asleep at all.

No. 17 PUB CRAWL

This problem is not very difficult if the inns are taken in the right order, which is: Blue Boar, Red Lion, Spotted Cow, Lamb, Fox and Hounds, Cat and Fiddle, White Hart, Black Horse, Pink Pig.

No. 18 FAITH, HOPE AND CHARITY

The only possible solution which complies with the condition of not passing along the same passages twice, and yet follows a consistent clue, is to take two right-hand turnings in succession and then two left-hand ones. Turnings are only reckoned where there is a choice of ways, and be it noted that a complete doubling back involves making *two* right-angled turns. Charity obtained the clue by underlining the *r*'s and *l*'s in the rhyme, which gave the succession: *rr, ll, rr, ll, rr, ll*, etc., etc.

No. 19 POUNDING THE BEAT

You start with a choice of the 4 ways numbered in the diagram. Take the first one: it leads to a choice of 3 ways. If you take the first of these you are led to a final choice of 2 ways. There are no other choices on this route, but you get the same number of choices whichever of the first four ways you start along, so the answer is: $4 \times 3 \times 2 = 24$.

No. 20 ALADDIN'S CAVE

No. 21 RAG-TIME BAND

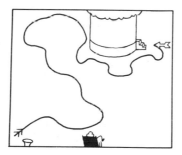

He need pass immediately in front of only one lady. There are 26 ladies present.

No. 22 DODGING THE MINES

If you start at Calais (which enables a clearer solution to be given), enter at the second gap from the left. The following instructions then apply only at those points where there is a choice of ways.

Ignore that right-hand turn, and then take the middle course where three ways meet; turn right round the "blind" and then left; ignore the right-hand turn and go straight up; ignore the next left-hand turn; after rounding the next "blind," take the second on the left; ignore the right-hand turn, and come out at the left-hand gap at Dover.

No. 23 YE GAME AND PLAYE OF YE "WOKKA"

The following moves will take each player "home" with 15 dominoes: 6–6, 6–3, 3–5, 5–1, 1–0, 0–2, 2–4, 4–5, 5–0, 0–3, 3–4, 4–1, 1–3, 3–0, 0–0. And: 1–1, 1–4, 4–3, 3–5, 5–4, 4–2, 2–1, 1–6, 6–3, 3–2, 2–5, 5–4, 4–2, 2–0, 0–0.

No. 24   ROSAMUND'S BOWER

You enter by the left-hand door, and turn immediately to the right. You then keep to the right till you find yourself more than half-way up the page, where there is a choice of two doors. Take the left-hand one, and at the next choice take the left-hand one also. And so may you pass along the top of the diagram to Rosamund's Bower. There are 50 rooms in this maze, 50 shut doors, and 50 open ones.

No. 25   THE MAZE OF THE MINOTAUR

The solution to this maze is really quite easy, once you know the way. And that is not a platitude. The maze has a horizontal "spoke" on the left-hand side running from the fifth line from the outer edge to the second line from the centre. If you draw a corresponding spoke on the right-hand side (from the second line from the centre to the fifth line from the outer edge) the maze is reduced to a single forced path, similar to the maze of Dedalus illustrated in Fig. 1.

No. 26   PUT YOUR FINGER IN MOUSIE'S HOLE

No. 27   THE TANGLED TELETAPE

Tape-reader 1 is looking at the wrong side, 2 and 3 at the right side.

No. 28   SEASIDE HOLIDAY

No. 1 can go to Rhyl, Tenby, Bournemouth.
No. 2 can go to Rhyl, Tenby, Bournemouth.
No. 3 can go to Eastbourne, Bournemouth.
No. 4 can go to Eastbourne, Bournemouth.
No. 5 can go to Deal.
No. 6 can go to Deal, Dunfermline, Hull, Fort William.
No. 7 can go to Deal, Dunfermline, Hull, Fort William.
No. 8 can go to Deal, Dunfermline, Hull, Fort William.
Nos. 1, 2, 3 and 4 therefore spent their holiday at Bournemouth, and Nos. 5, 6, 7 and 8 at Deal.

No. 29   THE TABLET OF FUM HOAM

Supposing section A to be in the right position with regard to the centre, B was dropped *in* half a turn, C is correct, and D was dropped *in* half a turn. If D or B is regarded as being correct, A and C must be held to have slipped *out* half a turn. Whichever way you look at it, you choose the inner path in passing from A to D, the outer path from D to C, the inner path from C to B, and the outer path from B to A.

No. 30   THE CASTLE MAZE

Since there is no way through the maze or *via* the rooms and passages, the King ought to have made use of the steps to the Dungeons. There are two flights of these, and he should have gone down one flight and come up the other. Sorry and all that!

No. 31   TREASURE ISLAND

The best way to the treasure is *via* the towns whose initial letters spell "THE BEST WAY." These are: The Haven, Hook Bay, Elftown, Brig Head, Edwardberg, Sand Creek, Thrums, Waterwell, Anchorville, Ye Treasure. That this is the shortest route may be seen with a map-measurer.

No. 32   THE KNIGHT'S TALE

Sir Jingo's yarn is read by performing the Knight's move (in Chess), so as to cover the whole board. The answer is: "'I know how he died,' said Sir Jingo Yarn. 'He was asleep during the sermon last Sunday morning, and dreamt that his creditors were after him. The worst among them, a man he had real cause to fear, was about to club his brains out when the parson thumped the pulpit. The effect was as if he had really been clubbed; he died instantly.' " The Inspector did not believe this yarn because, of course, if the Knight's uncle had died in his sleep in that way, how could Sir Jingo possibly have come to knowledge of his dream?

No. 33   THE CASTLE TELEPHONES

The course of the wires is as follows:

A—Right Lav., cross through Library, right up passage and past Study door.

B—Lobby, Waiting Room, Kitchen, Pantries, Outer Corridor.

C—Upper Gallery, second passage on right, round Kitchen, round Cellar stairs, Scullery, Verandah.

D—Lower Galley, Alcove.

E—Left Lav., Lounge, Dining Room, Sitting Room, passage to Cellars.

No. 34   GENTLEMEN OF THE ROAD

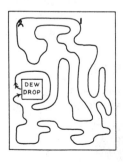

1. In this simplified diagram the numbers indicate the positions of the only two tramps you need to pass.

2. The continuous line passes all the tramps.

No. 35   THE PLUMBER'S PROBLEM

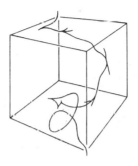

No. 36   SHOPPING DAY IN NEW YORK CITY

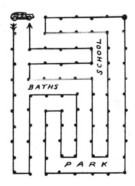

No. 37   PORTRAIT OF THE ARTIST AS A YOUNG MAN

The line beginning at "O" should, if traced correctly, come out at "8" at the top of the page. You may check it where it crosses the "obstacles" by means of a ruler, but in order to check the "steps" it is necessary to lay the ruler along them like a stair-carpet when the rods have come out, otherwise you will arrive at the wrong flight on the further side of the obstacle. Curves must be assumed to continue curving behind obstacles.

No. 38   EXTRA RUMMY

In the accompanying diagram R stands for a run, F for a flush, and P for a pair.

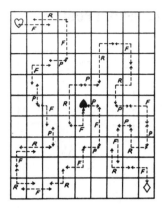

No. 39   GETTING THROUGH THE WIRE

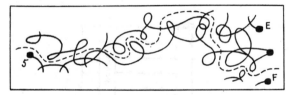

No. 40   HORRORSCOPE

Your natural course on entering this maze by the moon is to proceed towards the left — a tendency which the comets are supposed to enhance. But to solve the puzzle you must start the other way and go to the right. The solution may then be found by trial and error.

No. 41   THE ANSWER'S A ——!

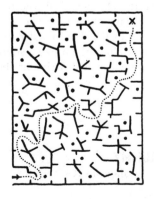

The maze in question is No. 20, "Aladdin's Cave," and on examination it will be apparent that these two mazes are the same except that one of them is "upside-down and wrong-way-round." This by no means implies that they are of equal difficulty. *That* depends largely on the person solving them.

No. 42   "SNAKES AND LADDERS"

1, 43, 46, 29, 16, 42, 5, 27, 21, 45, 14, 22, 31, 8, 38, 9, 2.

No. 43   ON THE TILES

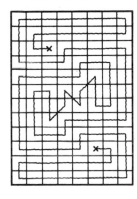

37 lines.   23 lines.

No. 44   KITTEN'S KNITTING

1 —Yellow.   2 — Brown.   3 — Blue.   4 — Red.   5 — Green.

No. 45   FUN WITH FUNGI

No. 46   ARCHIE THE ALCHEMIST

Lead — Tin — Iron — Brass — Gold.

No. 47   THE SHUNTER'S PROBLEM

Change from lines 1 to 3 (*middle of column*), from 3 to 10, from 10 to 8 (*middle*), from 8 to 7 (*top*), from 7 (*top*) to 7 (*bottom*), from 7 to 8 (*bottom*), from 8 to 11, from 11 to 10 (*bottom*), from 10 to 12, from 12 to 13 and 14 (*bottom*), from 14 to 12 (*middle*), from 12 to 14 (*top*), and from 14 to 15 (*top*). By going this way, Bill Buffer still had ten cars in his train.

No. 48   THE PHILADELPHIA MAZE

The answer is 640. The problem must be simplified before it can be solved, and H. E. Dudeney, the mathematical puzzle expert, reduced the essentials of this maze to the following diagram:

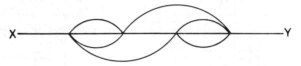

From this, it is not difficult to calculate the answer by the method used in No. 19, and those with sufficient patience can trace the 640 different routes from X to Y!

No. 49   THE SPIDER AND THE FLY

Since you must find this out by trial and error, you owe us a debt of gratitude for making you the Spider, and not the Fly!

No. 50   PIPS TO YOU!

This is another one — or rather, twelve — that you must work out for yourself.

A CATALOG OF SELECTED
DOVER BOOKS
IN ALL FIELDS OF INTEREST

A CATALOG OF SELECTED DOVER BOOKS IN ALL FIELDS OF INTEREST

CONCERNING THE SPIRITUAL IN ART, Wassily Kandinsky. Pioneering work by father of abstract art. Thoughts on color theory, nature of art. Analysis of earlier masters. 12 illustrations. 80pp. of text. 5⅜ × 8½. 23411-8 Pa. $2.95

LEONARDO ON THE HUMAN BODY, Leonardo da Vinci. More than 1200 of Leonardo's anatomical drawings on 215 plates. Leonardo's text, which accompanies the drawings, has been translated into English. 506pp. 8⅜ × 11¾. 24483-0 Pa. $11.95

GOBLIN MARKET, Christina Rossetti. Best-known work by poet comparable to Emily Dickinson, Alfred Tennyson. With 46 delightfully grotesque illustrations by Laurence Housman. 64pp. 4 × 6¾. 24516-0 Pa. $2.50

THE HEART OF THOREAU'S JOURNALS, edited by Odell Shepard. Selections from *Journal*, ranging over full gamut of interests. 228pp. 5⅜ × 8½. 20741-2 Pa. $4.50

MR. LINCOLN'S CAMERA MAN: MATHEW B. BRADY, Roy Meredith. Over 300 Brady photos reproduced directly from original negatives, photos. Lively commentary. 368pp. 8⅜ × 11¼. 23021-X Pa. $14.95

PHOTOGRAPHIC VIEWS OF SHERMAN'S CAMPAIGN, George N. Barnard. Reprint of landmark 1866 volume with 61 plates: battlefield of New Hope Church, the Etawah Bridge, the capture of Atlanta, etc. 80pp. 9 × 12. 23445-2 Pa. $6.00

A SHORT HISTORY OF ANATOMY AND PHYSIOLOGY FROM THE GREEKS TO HARVEY, Dr. Charles Singer. Thoroughly engrossing non-technical survey. 270 illustrations. 211pp. 5⅜ × 8½. 20389-1 Pa. $4.95

REDOUTE ROSES IRON-ON TRANSFER PATTERNS, Barbara Christopher. Redouté was botanical painter to the Empress Josephine; transfer his famous roses onto fabric with these 24 transfer patterns. 80pp. 8¼ × 10⅞. 24292-7 Pa. $3.50

THE FIVE BOOKS OF ARCHITECTURE, Sebastiano Serlio. Architectural milestone, first (1611) English translation of Renaissance classic. Unabridged reproduction of original edition includes over 300 woodcut illustrations. 416pp. 9⅜ × 12¼. 24349-4 Pa. $14.95

CARLSON'S GUIDE TO LANDSCAPE PAINTING, John F. Carlson. Authoritative, comprehensive guide covers, every aspect of landscape painting. 34 reproductions of paintings by author; 58 explanatory diagrams. 144pp. 8⅜ × 11. 22927-0 Pa. $5.95

101 PUZZLES IN THOUGHT AND LOGIC, C.R. Wylie, Jr. Solve murders, robberies, see which fishermen are liars—purely by reasoning! 107pp. 5⅜ × 8½. 20367-0 Pa. $2.00

TEST YOUR LOGIC, George J. Summers. 50 more truly new puzzles with new turns of thought, new subtleties of inference. 100pp. 5⅜ × 8½. 22877-0 Pa. $2.25

THE MURDER BOOK OF J.G. REEDER, Edgar Wallace. Eight suspenseful stories by bestselling mystery writer of 20s and 30s. Features the donnish Mr. J.G. Reeder of Public Prosecutor's Office. 128pp. 5⅜ × 8½. (Available in U.S. only)
24374-5 Pa. $3.95

ANNE ORR'S CHARTED DESIGNS, Anne Orr. Best designs by premier needlework designer, all on charts: flowers, borders, birds, children, alphabets, etc. Over 100 charts, 10 in color. Total of 40pp. 8¼ × 11. 23704-4 Pa. $2.50

BASIC CONSTRUCTION TECHNIQUES FOR HOUSES AND SMALL BUILDINGS SIMPLY EXPLAINED, U.S. Bureau of Naval Personnel. Grading, masonry, woodworking, floor and wall framing, roof framing, plastering, tile setting, much more. Over 675 illustrations. 568pp. 6½ × 9¼. 20242-9 Pa. $8.95

MATISSE LINE DRAWINGS AND PRINTS, Henri Matisse. Representative collection of female nudes, faces, still lifes, experimental works, etc., from 1898 to 1948. 50 illustrations. 48pp. 8⅜ × 11¼. 23877-6 Pa. $3.50

HOW TO PLAY THE CHESS OPENINGS, Eugene Znosko-Borovsky. Clear, profound examinations of just what each opening is intended to do and how opponent can counter. Many sample games. 147pp. 5⅜ × 8½. 22795-2 Pa. $2.95

DUPLICATE BRIDGE, Alfred Sheinwold. Clear, thorough, easily followed account: rules, etiquette, scoring, strategy, bidding; Goren's point-count system, Blackwood and Gerber conventions, etc. 158pp. 5⅜ × 8½. 22741-3 Pa. $3.00

SARGENT PORTRAIT DRAWINGS, J.S. Sargent. Collection of 42 portraits reveals technical skill and intuitive eye of noted American portrait painter, John Singer Sargent. 48pp. 8¼ × 11⅛. 24524-1 Pa. $3.50

ENTERTAINING SCIENCE EXPERIMENTS WITH EVERYDAY OBJECTS, Martin Gardner. Over 100 experiments for youngsters. Will amuse, astonish, teach, and entertain. Over 100 illustrations. 127pp. 5⅜ × 8½. 24201-3 Pa. $2.50

TEDDY BEAR PAPER DOLLS IN FULL COLOR: A Family of Four Bears and Their Costumes, Crystal Collins. A family of four Teddy Bear paper dolls and nearly 60 cut-out costumes. Full color, printed one side only. 32pp. 9¼ × 12¼. 24550-0 Pa. $3.50

NEW CALLIGRAPHIC ORNAMENTS AND FLOURISHES, Arthur Baker. Unusual, multi-useable material: arrows, pointing hands, brackets and frames, ovals, swirls, birds, etc. Nearly 700 illustrations. 80pp. 8⅜ × 11¼. 24095-9 Pa. $3.75

DINOSAUR DIORAMAS TO CUT & ASSEMBLE, M. Kalmenoff. Two complete three-dimensional scenes in full color, with 31 cut-out animals and plants. Excellent educational toy for youngsters. Instructions; 2 assembly diagrams. 32pp. 9¼ × 12¼. 24541-1 Pa. $4.50

SILHOUETTES: A PICTORIAL ARCHIVE OF VARIED ILLUSTRATIONS, edited by Carol Belanger Grafton. Over 600 silhouettes from the 18th to 20th centuries. Profiles and full figures of men, women, children, birds, animals, groups and scenes, nature, ships, an alphabet. 144pp. 8⅜ × 11¼. 23781-8 Pa. $5.95

25 KITES THAT FLY, Leslie Hunt. Full, easy-to-follow instructions for kites made from inexpensive materials. Many novelties. 70 illustrations. 110pp. 5⅜ × 8½.
22550-X Pa. $2.50

PIANO TUNING, J. Cree Fischer. Clearest, best book for beginner, amateur. Simple repairs, raising dropped notes, tuning by easy method of flattened fifths. No previous skills needed. 4 illustrations. 201pp. 5⅜ × 8½. 23267-0 Pa. $3.50

EARLY AMERICAN IRON-ON TRANSFER PATTERNS, edited by Rita Weiss. 75 designs, borders, alphabets, from traditional American sources. 48pp. 8¼ × 11.
23162-3 Pa. $1.95

CROCHETING EDGINGS, edited by Rita Weiss. Over 100 of the best designs for these lovely trims for a host of household items. Complete instructions, illustrations. 48pp. 8¼ × 11. 24031-2 Pa. $2.25

FINGER PLAYS FOR NURSERY AND KINDERGARTEN, Emilie Poulsson. 18 finger plays with music (voice and piano); entertaining, instructive. Counting, nature lore, etc. Victorian classic. 53 illustrations. 80pp. 6½ × 9¼. 22588-7 Pa. $1.95

BOSTON THEN AND NOW, Peter Vanderwarker. Here in 59 side-by-side views are photographic documentations of the city's past and present. 119 photographs. Full captions. 122pp. 8¼ × 11. 24312-5 Pa. $7.95

CROCHETING BEDSPREADS, edited by Rita Weiss. 22 patterns, originally published in three instruction books 1939-41. 39 photos, 8 charts. Instructions. 48pp. 8¼ × 11. 23610-2 Pa. $2.00

HAWTHORNE ON PAINTING, Charles W. Hawthorne. Collected from notes taken by students at famous Cape Cod School; hundreds of direct, personal *apercus*, ideas, suggestions. 91pp. 5⅜ × 8½. 20653-X Pa. $2.95

THERMODYNAMICS, Enrico Fermi. A classic of modern science. Clear, organized treatment of systems, first and second laws, entropy, thermodynamic potentials, etc. Calculus required. 160pp. 5⅜ × 8½. 60361-X Pa. $4.50

TEN BOOKS ON ARCHITECTURE, Vitruvius. The most important book ever written on architecture. Early Roman aesthetics, technology, classical orders, site selection, all other aspects. Morgan translation. 331pp. 5⅜ × 8½. 20645-9 Pa. $5.95

THE CORNELL BREAD BOOK, Clive M. McCay and Jeanette B. McCay. Famed high-protein recipe incorporated into breads, rolls, buns, coffee cakes, pizza, pie crusts, more. Nearly 50 illustrations. 48pp. 8¼ × 11. 23995-0 Pa. $2.00

THE CRAFTSMAN'S HANDBOOK, Cennino Cennini. 15th-century handbook, school of Giotto, explains applying gold, silver leaf; gesso; fresco painting, grinding pigments, etc. 142pp. 6⅛ × 9¼. 20054-X Pa. $3.50

FRANK LLOYD WRIGHT'S FALLINGWATER, Donald Hoffmann. Full story of Wright's masterwork at Bear Run, Pa. 100 photographs of site, construction, and details of completed structure. 112pp. 9¼ × 10. 23671-4 Pa. $7.95

OVAL STAINED GLASS PATTERN BOOK, C. Eaton. 60 new designs framed in shape of an oval. Greater complexity, challenge with sinuous cats, birds, mandalas framed in antique shape. 64pp. 8¼ × 11. 24519-5 Pa. $3.75

THE BOOK OF WOOD CARVING, Charles Marshall Sayers. Still finest book for beginning student. Fundamentals, technique; gives 34 designs, over 34 projects for panels, bookends, mirrors, etc. 33 photos. 118pp. 7¾ × 10⅝. 23654-4 Pa. $3.95

CARVING COUNTRY CHARACTERS, Bill Higginbotham. Expert advice for beginning, advanced carvers on materials, techniques for creating 18 projects—mirthful panorama of American characters. 105 illustrations. 80pp. 8⅜ × 11. 24135-1 Pa. $2.50

300 ART NOUVEAU DESIGNS AND MOTIFS IN FULL COLOR, C.B. Grafton. 44 full-page plates display swirling lines and muted colors typical of Art Nouveau. Borders, frames, panels, cartouches, dingbats, etc. 48pp. 9⅜ × 12¼. 24354-0 Pa. $6.95

SELF-WORKING CARD TRICKS, Karl Fulves. Editor of *Pallbearer* offers 72 tricks that work automatically through nature of card deck. No sleight of hand needed. Often spectacular. 42 illustrations. 113pp. 5⅜ × 8½. 23334-0 Pa. $3.50

CUT AND ASSEMBLE A WESTERN FRONTIER TOWN, Edmund V. Gillon, Jr. Ten authentic full-color buildings on heavy cardboard stock in H-O scale. Sheriff's Office and Jail, Saloon, Wells Fargo, Opera House, others. 48pp. 9¼ × 12¼. 23736-2 Pa. $4.95

CUT AND ASSEMBLE AN EARLY NEW ENGLAND VILLAGE, Edmund V. Gillon, Jr. Printed in full color on heavy cardboard stock. 12 authentic buildings in H-O scale: Adams home in Quincy, Mass., Oliver Wight house in Sturbridge, smithy, store, church, others. 48pp. 9¼ × 12¼. 23536-X Pa. $4.95

THE TALE OF TWO BAD MICE, Beatrix Potter. Tom Thumb and Hunca Munca squeeze out of their hole and go exploring. 27 full-color Potter illustrations. 59pp. 4¼ × 5½. (Available in U.S. only) 23065-1 Pa. $1.75

CARVING FIGURE CARICATURES IN THE OZARK STYLE, Harold L. Enlow. Instructions and illustrations for ten delightful projects, plus general carving instructions. 22 drawings and 47 photographs altogether. 39pp. 8⅜ × 11. 23151-8 Pa. $2.95

A TREASURY OF FLOWER DESIGNS FOR ARTISTS, EMBROIDERERS AND CRAFTSMEN, Susan Gaber. 100 garden favorites lushly rendered by artist for artists, craftsmen, needleworkers. Many form frames, borders. 80pp. 8¼ × 11. 24096-7 Pa. $3.50

CUT & ASSEMBLE A TOY THEATER/THE NUTCRACKER BALLET, Tom Tierney. Model of a complete, full-color production of Tchaikovsky's classic. 6 backdrops, dozens of characters, familiar dance sequences. 32pp. 9⅜ × 12¼. 24194-7 Pa. $4.50

ANIMALS: 1,419 COPYRIGHT-FREE ILLUSTRATIONS OF MAMMALS, BIRDS, FISH, INSECTS, ETC., edited by Jim Harter. Clear wood engravings present, in extremely lifelike poses, over 1,000 species of animals. 284pp. 9 × 12. 23766-4 Pa. $9.95

MORE HAND SHADOWS, Henry Bursill. For those at their 'finger ends," 16 more effects—Shakespeare, a hare, a squirrel, Mr. Punch, and twelve more—each explained by a full-page illustration. Considerable period charm. 30pp. 6½ × 9¼. 21384-6 Pa. $1.95

SURREAL STICKERS AND UNREAL STAMPS, William Rowe. 224 haunting, hilarious stamps on gummed, perforated stock, with images of elephants, geisha girls, George Washington, etc. 16pp. one side. 8¼ × 11.   24371-0 Pa. $3.50

GOURMET KITCHEN LABELS, Ed Sibbett, Jr. 112 full-color labels (4 copies each of 28 designs). Fruit, bread, other culinary motifs. Gummed and perforated. 16pp. 8¼ × 11.   24087-8 Pa. $2.95

PATTERNS AND INSTRUCTIONS FOR CARVING AUTHENTIC BIRDS, H.D. Green. Detailed instructions, 27 diagrams, 85 photographs for carving 15 species of birds so life-like, they'll seem ready to fly! 8¼ × 11.   24222-6 Pa. $2.75

FLATLAND, E.A. Abbott. Science-fiction classic explores life of 2-D being in 3-D world. 16 illustrations. 103pp. 5⅜ × 8.   20001-9 Pa. $2.00

DRIED FLOWERS, Sarah Whitlock and Martha Rankin. Concise, clear, practical guide to dehydration, glycerinizing, pressing plant material, and more. Covers use of silica gel. 12 drawings. 32pp. 5⅜ × 8½.   21802-3 Pa. $1.00

EASY-TO-MAKE CANDLES, Gary V. Guy. Learn how easy it is to make all kinds of decorative candles. Step-by-step instructions. 82 illustrations. 48pp. 8¼ × 11.   23881-4 Pa. $2.95

SUPER STICKERS FOR KIDS, Carolyn Bracken. 128 gummed and perforated full-color stickers: GIRL WANTED, KEEP OUT, BORED OF EDUCATION, X-RATED, COMBAT ZONE, many others. 16pp. 8¼ × 11.   24092-4 Pa. $2.50

CUT AND COLOR PAPER MASKS, Michael Grater. Clowns, animals, funny faces...simply color them in, cut them out, and put them together, and you have 9 paper masks to play with and enjoy. 32pp. 8¼ × 11.   23171-2 Pa. $2.50

A CHRISTMAS CAROL: THE ORIGINAL MANUSCRIPT, Charles Dickens. Clear facsimile of Dickens manuscript, on facing pages with final printed text. 8 illustrations by John Leech, 4 in color on covers. 144pp. 8⅜ × 11¼.   20980-6 Pa. $5.95

CARVING SHOREBIRDS, Harry V. Shourds & Anthony Hillman. 16 full-size patterns (all double-page spreads) for 19 North American shorebirds with step-by-step instructions. 72pp. 9¼ × 12¼.   24287-0 Pa. $4.95

THE GENTLE ART OF MATHEMATICS, Dan Pedoe. Mathematical games, probability, the question of infinity, topology, how the laws of algebra work, problems of irrational numbers, and more. 42 figures. 143pp. 5⅜ × 8½. (EBE)   22949-1 Pa. $3.50

READY-TO-USE DOLLHOUSE WALLPAPER, Katzenbach & Warren, Inc. Stripe, 2 floral stripes, 2 allover florals, polka dot; all in full color. 4 sheets (350 sq. in.) of each, enough for average room. 48pp. 8¼ × 11.   23495-9 Pa. $2.95

MINIATURE IRON-ON TRANSFER PATTERNS FOR DOLLHOUSES, DOLLS, AND SMALL PROJECTS, Rita Weiss and Frank Fontana. Over 100 miniature patterns: rugs, bedspreads, quilts, chair seats, etc. In standard dollhouse size. 48pp. 8¼ × 11.   23741-9 Pa. $1.95

THE DINOSAUR COLORING BOOK, Anthony Rao. 45 renderings of dinosaurs, fossil birds, turtles, other creatures of Mesozoic Era. Scientifically accurate. Captions. 48pp. 8¼ × 11.   24022-3 Pa. $2.50

JAPANESE DESIGN MOTIFS, Matsuya Co. Mon, or heraldic designs. Over 4000 typical, beautiful designs: birds, animals, flowers, swords, fans, geometrics; all beautifully stylized. 213pp. 11⅜ × 8¼. 22874-6 Pa. $7.95

THE TALE OF BENJAMIN BUNNY, Beatrix Potter. Peter Rabbit's cousin coaxes him back into Mr. McGregor's garden for a whole new set of adventures. All 27 full-color illustrations. 59pp. 4¼ × 5½. (Available in U.S. only) 21102-9 Pa. $1.75

THE TALE OF PETER RABBIT AND OTHER FAVORITE STORIES BOXED SET, Beatrix Potter. Seven of Beatrix Potter's best-loved tales including Peter Rabbit in a specially designed, durable boxed set. 4¼ × 5½. Total of 447pp. 158 color illustrations. (Available in U.S. only) 23903-9 Pa. $12.25

PRACTICAL MENTAL MAGIC, Theodore Annemann. Nearly 200 astonishing feats of mental magic revealed in step-by-step detail. Complete advice on staging, patter, etc. Illustrated. 320pp. 5⅜ × 8½. 24426-1 Pa. $5.95

CELEBRATED CASES OF JUDGE DEE (DEE GOONG AN), translated by Robert Van Gulik. Authentic 18th-century Chinese detective novel; Dee and associates solve three interlocked cases. Led to van Gulik's own stories with same characters. Extensive introduction. 9 illustrations. 237pp. 5⅜ × 8½.
23337-5 Pa. $4.95

CUT & FOLD EXTRATERRESTRIAL INVADERS THAT FLY, M. Grater. Stage your own lilliputian space battles.By following the step-by-step instructions and explanatory diagrams you can launch 22 full-color fliers into space. 36pp. 8¼ × 11. 24478-4 Pa. $2.95

CUT & ASSEMBLE VICTORIAN HOUSES, Edmund V. Gillon, Jr. Printed in full color on heavy cardboard stock, 4 authentic Victorian houses in H-O scale: Italian-style Villa, Octagon, Second Empire, Stick Style. 48pp. 9¼ × 12¼.
23849-0 Pa. $4.95

BEST SCIENCE FICTION STORIES OF H.G. WELLS, H.G. Wells. Full novel The Invisible Man, plus 17 short stories: "The Crystal Egg," "Aepyornis Island," "The Strange Orchid," etc. 303pp. 5⅜ × 8½. (Available in U.S. only)
21531-8 Pa. $4.95

TRADEMARK DESIGNS OF THE WORLD, Yusaku Kamekura. A lavish collection of nearly 700 trademarks, the work of Wright, Loewy, Klee, Binder, hundreds of others. 160pp. 8¾ × 8. (Available in U.S. only) (EJ) 24191-2 Pa. $5.95

THE ARTIST'S AND CRAFTSMAN'S GUIDE TO REDUCING, ENLARGING AND TRANSFERRING DESIGNS, Rita Weiss. Discover, reduce, enlarge, transfer designs from any objects to any craft project. 12pp. plus 16 sheets special graph paper. 8¼ × 11. 24142-4 Pa. $3.50

TREASURY OF JAPANESE DESIGNS AND MOTIFS FOR ARTISTS AND CRAFTSMEN, edited by Carol Belanger Grafton. Indispensable collection of 360 traditional Japanese designs and motifs redrawn in clean, crisp black-and-white, copyright-free illustrations. 96pp. 8¼ × 11. 24435-0 Pa. $3.95

CHANCERY CURSIVE STROKE BY STROKE, Arthur Baker. Instructions and illustrations for each stroke of each letter (upper and lower case) and numerals. 54 full-page plates. 64pp. 8¼ × 11. 24278-1 Pa. $2.50

THE ENJOYMENT AND USE OF COLOR, Walter Sargent. Color relationships, values, intensities; complementary colors, illumination, similar topics. Color in nature and art. 7 color plates, 29 illustrations. 274pp. 5⅜ × 8½. 20944-X Pa. $4.95

SCULPTURE PRINCIPLES AND PRACTICE, Louis Slobodkin. Step-by-step approach to clay, plaster, metals, stone; classical and modern. 253 drawings, photos. 255pp. 8⅛ × 11. 22960-2 Pa. $7.50

VICTORIAN FASHION PAPER DOLLS FROM HARPER'S BAZAR, 1867-1898, Theodore Menten. Four female dolls with 28 elegant high fashion costumes, printed in full color. 32pp. 9¼ × 12¼. (USCO) 23453-3 Pa. $3.95

FLOPSY, MOPSY AND COTTONTAIL: A Little Book of Paper Dolls in Full Color, Susan LaBelle. Three dolls and 21 costumes (7 for each doll) show Peter Rabbit's siblings dressed for holidays, gardening, hiking, etc. Charming borders, captions. 48pp. 4¼ × 5½. 24376-1 Pa. $2.50

NATIONAL LEAGUE BASEBALL CARD CLASSICS, Bert Randolph Sugar. 83 big-leaguers from 1909-69 on facsimile cards. Hubbell, Dean, Spahn, Brock plus advertising, info, no duplications. Perforated, detachable. 16pp. 8¼ × 11.
24308-7 Pa. $2.95

THE LOGICAL APPROACH TO CHESS, Dr. Max Euwe, et al. First-rate text of comprehensive strategy, tactics, theory for the amateur. No gambits to memorize, just a clear, logical approach. 224pp. 5⅜ × 8½. 24353-2 Pa. $4.50

MAGICK IN THEORY AND PRACTICE, Aleister Crowley. The summation of the thought and practice of the century's most famous necromancer, long hard to find. Crowley's best book. 436pp. 5⅜ × 8½. (Available in U.S. only)
23295-6 Pa. $6.50

THE HAUNTED HOTEL, Wilkie Collins. Collins' last great tale; doom and destiny in a Venetian palace. Praised by T.S. Eliot. 127pp. 5⅜ × 8½.
24333-8 Pa. $3.00

ART DECO DISPLAY ALPHABETS, Dan X. Solo. Wide variety of bold yet elegant lettering in handsome Art Deco styles. 100 complete fonts, with numerals, punctuation, more. 104pp. 8⅛ × 11. 24372-9 Pa. $4.50

CALLIGRAPHIC ALPHABETS, Arthur Baker. Nearly 150 complete alphabets by outstanding contemporary. Stimulating ideas; useful source for unique effects. 154 plates. 157pp. 8⅜ × 11¼. 21045-6 Pa. $5.95

ARTHUR BAKER'S HISTORIC CALLIGRAPHIC ALPHABETS, Arthur Baker. From monumental capitals of first-century Rome to humanistic cursive of 16th century, 33 alphabets in fresh interpretations. 88 plates. 96pp. 9 × 12.
24054-1 Pa. $4.50

LETTIE LANE PAPER DOLLS, Sheila Young. Genteel turn-of-the-century family very popular then and now. 24 paper dolls. 16 plates in full color. 32pp. 9¼ × 12¼. 24089-4 Pa. $3.50

KEYBOARD WORKS FOR SOLO INSTRUMENTS, G.F. Handel. 35 neglected works from Handel's vast oeuvre, originally jotted down as improvisations. Includes Eight Great Suites, others. New sequence. 174pp. 9⅜ × 12¼.
24338-9 Pa. $7.50

AMERICAN LEAGUE BASEBALL CARD CLASSICS, Bert Randolph Sugar. 82 stars from 1900s to 60s on facsimile cards. Ruth, Cobb, Mantle, Williams, plus advertising, info, no duplications. Perforated, detachable. 16pp. 8¼ × 11.
24286-2 Pa. $2.95

A TREASURY OF CHARTED DESIGNS FOR NEEDLEWORKERS, Georgia Gorham and Jeanne Warth. 141 charted designs: owl, cat with yarn, tulips, piano, spinning wheel, covered bridge, Victorian house and many others. 48pp. 8¼ × 11.
23558-0 Pa. $1.95

DANISH FLORAL CHARTED DESIGNS, Gerda Bengtsson. Exquisite collection of over 40 different florals: anemone, Iceland poppy, wild fruit, pansies, many others. 45 illustrations. 48pp. 8¼ × 11.
23957-8 Pa. $1.95

OLD PHILADELPHIA IN EARLY PHOTOGRAPHS 1839-1914, Robert F. Looney. 215 photographs: panoramas, street scenes, landmarks, President-elect Lincoln's visit, 1876 Centennial Exposition, much more. 230pp. 8⅜ × 11¾.
23345-6 Pa. $9.95

PRELUDE TO MATHEMATICS, W.W. Sawyer. Noted mathematician's lively, stimulating account of non-Euclidean geometry, matrices, determinants, group theory, other topics. Emphasis on novel, striking aspects. 224pp. 5⅜ × 8½.
24401-6 Pa. $4.50

ADVENTURES WITH A MICROSCOPE, Richard Headstrom. 59 adventures with clothing fibers, protozoa, ferns and lichens, roots and leaves, much more. 142 illustrations. 232pp. 5⅜ × 8½.
23471-1 Pa. $3.95

IDENTIFYING ANIMAL TRACKS: MAMMALS, BIRDS, AND OTHER ANIMALS OF THE EASTERN UNITED STATES, Richard Headstrom. For hunters, naturalists, scouts, nature-lovers. Diagrams of tracks, tips on identification. 128pp. 5⅜ × 8.
24442-3 Pa. $3.50

VICTORIAN FASHIONS AND COSTUMES FROM HARPER'S BAZAR, 1867-1898, edited by Stella Blum. Day costumes, evening wear, sports clothes, shoes, hats, other accessories in over 1,000 detailed engravings. 320pp. 9⅜ × 12¼.
22990-4 Pa. $10.95

EVERYDAY FASHIONS OF THE TWENTIES AS PICTURED IN SEARS AND OTHER CATALOGS, edited by Stella Blum. Actual dress of the Roaring Twenties, with text by Stella Blum. Over 750 illustrations, captions. 156pp. 9 × 12.
24134-3 Pa. $8.50

HALL OF FAME BASEBALL CARDS, edited by Bert Randolph Sugar. Cy Young, Ted Williams, Lou Gehrig, and many other Hall of Fame greats on 92 full-color, detachable reprints of early baseball cards. No duplication of cards with *Classic Baseball Cards*. 16pp. 8¼ × 11.
23624-2 Pa. $3.50

THE ART OF HAND LETTERING, Helm Wotzkow. Course in hand lettering, Roman, Gothic, Italic, Block, Script. Tools, proportions, optical aspects, individual variation. Very quality conscious. Hundreds of specimens. 320pp. 5⅜ × 8½.
21797-3 Pa. $4.95

HOW THE OTHER HALF LIVES, Jacob A. Riis. Journalistic record of filth, degradation, upward drive in New York immigrant slums, shops, around 1900. New edition includes 100 original Riis photos, monuments of early photography. 233pp. 10 × 7⅞. 22012-5 Pa. $7.95

CHINA AND ITS PEOPLE IN EARLY PHOTOGRAPHS, John Thomson. In 200 black-and-white photographs of exceptional quality photographic pioneer Thomson captures the mountains, dwellings, monuments and people of 19th-century China. 272pp. 9⅜ × 12¼. 24393-1 Pa. $13.95

GODEY COSTUME PLATES IN COLOR FOR DECOUPAGE AND FRAMING, edited by Eleanor Hasbrouk Rawlings. 24 full-color engravings depicting 19th-century Parisian haute couture. Printed on one side only. 56pp. 8¼ × 11. 23879-2 Pa. $3.95

ART NOUVEAU STAINED GLASS PATTERN BOOK, Ed Sibbett, Jr. 104 projects using well-known themes of Art Nouveau: swirling forms, florals, peacocks, and sensuous women. 60pp. 8¼ × 11. 23577-7 Pa. $3.50

QUICK AND EASY PATCHWORK ON THE SEWING MACHINE: Susan Aylsworth Murwin and Suzzy Payne. Instructions, diagrams show exactly how to machine sew 12 quilts. 48pp. of templates. 50 figures. 80pp. 8¼ × 11. 23770-2 Pa. $3.50

THE STANDARD BOOK OF QUILT MAKING AND COLLECTING, Marguerite Ickis. Full information, full-sized patterns for making 46 traditional quilts, also 150 other patterns. 483 illustrations. 273pp. 6⅞ × 9⅝. 20582-7 Pa. $5.95

LETTERING AND ALPHABETS, J. Albert Cavanagh. 85 complete alphabets lettered in various styles; instructions for spacing, roughs, brushwork. 121pp. 8¾ × 8. 20053-1 Pa. $3.95

LETTER FORMS: 110 COMPLETE ALPHABETS, Frederick Lambert. 110 sets of capital letters; 16 lower case alphabets; 70 sets of numbers and other symbols. 110pp. 8⅛ × 11. 22872-X Pa. $4.50

ORCHIDS AS HOUSE PLANTS, Rebecca Tyson Northen. Grow cattleyas and many other kinds of orchids—in a window, in a case, or under artificial light. 63 illustrations. 148pp. 5⅜ × 8½. 23261-1 Pa. $2.95

THE MUSHROOM HANDBOOK, Louis C.C. Krieger. Still the best popular handbook. Full descriptions of 259 species, extremely thorough text, poisons, folklore, etc. 32 color plates; 126 other illustrations. 560pp. 5⅜ × 8½. 21861-9 Pa. $8.50

THE DORÉ BIBLE ILLUSTRATIONS, Gustave Doré. All wonderful, detailed plates: Adam and Eve, Flood, Babylon, life of Jesus, etc. Brief King James text with each plate. 241 plates. 241pp. 9 × 12. 23004-X Pa. $8.95

THE BOOK OF KELLS: Selected Plates in Full Color, edited by Blanche Cirker. 32 full-page plates from greatest manuscript-icon of early Middle Ages. Fantastic, mysterious. Publisher's Note. Captions. 32pp. 9¾ × 12¼. 24345-1 Pa. $4.50

THE PERFECT WAGNERITE, George Bernard Shaw. Brilliant criticism of the Ring Cycle, with provocative interpretation of politics, economic theories behind the Ring. 136pp. 5⅜ × 8½. (EUK) 21707-8 Pa. $3.00

THE RIME OF THE ANCIENT MARINER, Gustave Doré, S.T. Coleridge. Doré's finest work, 34 plates capture moods, subtleties of poem. Full text. 77pp. 9¼ × 12.   22305-1 Pa. $4.95

SONGS OF INNOCENCE, William Blake. The first and most popular of Blake's famous "Illuminated Books," in a facsimile edition reproducing all 31 brightly colored plates. Additional printed text of each poem. 64pp. 5¼ × 7.
                                                                22764-2 Pa. $3.50

AN INTRODUCTION TO INFORMATION THEORY, J.R. Pierce. Second (1980) edition of most impressive non-technical account available. Encoding, entropy, noisy channel, related areas, etc. 320pp. 5⅜ × 8½.   24061-4 Pa. $4.95

THE DIVINE PROPORTION: A STUDY IN MATHEMATICAL BEAUTY, H.E. Huntley. "Divine proportion" or "golden ratio" in poetry, Pascal's triangle, philosophy, psychology, music, mathematical figures, etc. Excellent bridge between science and art. 58 figures. 185pp. 5⅜ × 8½.   22254-3 Pa. $3.95

THE DOVER NEW YORK WALKING GUIDE: From the Battery to Wall Street, Mary J. Shapiro. Superb inexpensive guide to historic buildings and locales in lower Manhattan: Trinity Church, Bowling Green, more. Complete Text; maps. 36 illustrations. 48pp. 3⅞ × 9¼.   24225-0 Pa. $2.50

NEW YORK THEN AND NOW, Edward B. Watson, Edmund V. Gillon, Jr. 83 important Manhattan sites: on facing pages early photographs (1875-1925) and 1976 photos by Gillon. 172 illustrations. 171pp. 9¼ × 10.   23361-8 Pa. $9.95

HISTORIC COSTUME IN PICTURES, Braun & Schneider. Over 1450 costumed figures from dawn of civilization to end of 19th century. English captions. 125 plates. 256pp. 8⅜ × 11¼.   23150-X Pa. $7.50

VICTORIAN AND EDWARDIAN FASHION: A Photographic Survey, Alison Gernsheim. First fashion history completely illustrated by contemporary photographs. Full text plus 235 photos, 1840-1914, in which many celebrities appear. 240pp. 6½ × 9¼.   24205-6 Pa. $6.00

CHARTED CHRISTMAS DESIGNS FOR COUNTED CROSS-STITCH AND OTHER NEEDLECRAFTS, Lindberg Press. Charted designs for 45 beautiful needlecraft projects with many yuletide and wintertime motifs. 48pp. 8¼ × 11. (EDNS)   24356-7 Pa. $2.50

101 FOLK DESIGNS FOR COUNTED CROSS-STITCH AND OTHER NEEDLE-CRAFTS, Carter Houck. 101 authentic charted folk designs in a wide array of lovely representations with many suggestions for effective use. 48pp. 8¼ × 11.
                                                                24369-9 Pa. $2.25

FIVE ACRES AND INDEPENDENCE, Maurice G. Kains. Great back-to-the-land classic explains basics of self-sufficient farming. The one book to get. 95 illustrations. 397pp. 5⅜ × 8½.   20974-1 Pa. $5.95

A MODERN HERBAL, Margaret Grieve. Much the fullest, most exact, most useful compilation of herbal material. Gigantic alphabetical encyclopedia, from aconite to zedoary, gives botanical information, medical properties, folklore, economic uses, and much else. Indispensable to serious reader. 161 illustrations. 888pp. 6½ × 9¼. (Available in U.S. only)   22798-7, 22799-5 Pa., Two-vol. set $16.45

DECORATIVE NAPKIN FOLDING FOR BEGINNERS, Lillian Oppenheimer and Natalie Epstein. 22 different napkin folds in the shape of a heart, clown's hat, love knot, etc. 63 drawings. 48pp. 8¼ × 11. 23797-4 Pa. $1.95

DECORATIVE LABELS FOR HOME CANNING, PRESERVING, AND OTHER HOUSEHOLD AND GIFT USES, Theodore Menten. 128 gummed, perforated labels, beautifully printed in 2 colors. 12 versions. Adhere to metal, glass, wood, ceramics. 24pp. 8¼ × 11. 23219-0 Pa. $3.50

EARLY AMERICAN STENCILS ON WALLS AND FURNITURE, Janet Waring. Thorough coverage of 19th-century folk art: techniques, artifacts, surviving specimens. 166 illustrations, 7 in color. 147pp. of text. 7⅞ × 10¾. 21906-2 Pa. $9.95

AMERICAN ANTIQUE WEATHERVANES, A.B. & W.T. Westervelt. Extensively illustrated 1883 catalog exhibiting over 550 copper weathervanes and finials. Excellent primary source by one of the principal manufacturers. 104pp. 6⅛ × 9¼. 24396-6 Pa. $3.95

ART STUDENTS' ANATOMY, Edmond J. Farris. Long favorite in art schools. Basic elements, common positions, actions. Full text, 158 illustrations. 159pp. 5⅜ × 8½. 20744-7 Pa. $3.95

BRIDGMAN'S LIFE DRAWING, George B. Bridgman. More than 500 drawings and text teach you to abstract the body into its major masses. Also specific areas of anatomy. 192pp. 6½ × 9¼. (EA) 22710-3 Pa. $4.50

COMPLETE PRELUDES AND ETUDES FOR SOLO PIANO, Frederic Chopin. All 26 Preludes, all 27 Etudes by greatest composer of piano music. Authoritative Paderewski edition. 224pp. 9 × 12. (Available in U.S. only) 24052-5 Pa. $7.50

PIANO MUSIC 1888-1905, Claude Debussy. Deux Arabesques, Suite Bergamesque, Masques, 1st series of Images, etc. 9 others, in corrected editions. 175pp. 9⅜ × 12¼. 22771-5 Pa. $5.95

TEDDY BEAR IRON-ON TRANSFER PATTERNS, Ted Menten. 80 iron-on transfer patterns of male and female Teddys in a wide variety of activities, poses, sizes. 48pp. 8¼ × 11. 24596-9 Pa. $2.25

A PICTURE HISTORY OF THE BROOKLYN BRIDGE, M.J. Shapiro. Profusely illustrated account of greatest engineering achievement of 19th century. 167 rare photos & engravings recall construction, human drama. Extensive, detailed text. 122pp. 8¼ × 11. 24403-2 Pa. $7.95

NEW YORK IN THE THIRTIES, Berenice Abbott. Noted photographer's fascinating study shows new buildings that have become famous and old sights that have disappeared forever. 97 photographs. 97pp. 11⅜ × 10. 22967-X Pa. $7.50

MATHEMATICAL TABLES AND FORMULAS, Robert D. Carmichael and Edwin R. Smith. Logarithms, sines, tangents, trig functions, powers, roots, reciprocals, exponential and hyperbolic functions, formulas and theorems. 269pp. 5⅜ × 8½. 60111-0 Pa. $4.95

HANDBOOK OF MATHEMATICAL FUNCTIONS WITH FORMULAS, GRAPHS, AND MATHEMATICAL TABLES, edited by Milton Abramowitz and Irene A. Stegun. Vast compendium: 29 sets of tables, some to as high as 20 places. 1,046pp. 8 × 10½. 61272-4 Pa. $19.95

REASON IN ART, George Santayana. Renowned philosopher's provocative, seminal treatment of basis of art in instinct and experience. Volume Four of *The Life of Reason*. 230pp. 5⅜ × 8. 24358-3 Pa. $4.50

LANGUAGE, TRUTH AND LOGIC, Alfred J. Ayer. Famous, clear introduction to Vienna, Cambridge schools of Logical Positivism. Role of philosophy, elimination of metaphysics, nature of analysis, etc. 160pp. 5⅜ × 8½. (USCO) 20010-8 Pa. $2.95

BASIC ELECTRONICS, U.S. Bureau of Naval Personnel. Electron tubes, circuits, antennas, AM, FM, and CW transmission and receiving, etc. 560 illustrations. 567pp. 6½ × 9¼. 21076-6 Pa. $8.95

THE ART DECO STYLE, edited by Theodore Menten. Furniture, jewelry, metalwork, ceramics, fabrics, lighting fixtures, interior decors, exteriors, graphics from pure French sources. Over 400 photographs. 183pp. 8⅜ × 11¼. 22824-X Pa. $7.95

THE FOUR BOOKS OF ARCHITECTURE, Andrea Palladio. 16th-century classic covers classical architectural remains, Renaissance revivals, classical orders, etc. 1738 Ware English edition. 216 plates. 110pp. of text. 9½ × 12¾ 21308-0 Pa. $11.50

THE WIT AND HUMOR OF OSCAR WILDE, edited by Alvin Redman. More than 1000 ripostes, paradoxes, wisecracks: Work is the curse of the drinking classes, I can resist everything except temptations, etc. 258pp. 5⅜ × 8½. 20602-5 Pa. $3.95

THE DEVIL'S DICTIONARY, Ambrose Bierce. Barbed, bitter, brilliant witticisms in the form of a dictionary. Best, most ferocious satire America has produced. 145pp. 5⅜ × 8½. 20487-1 Pa. $2.75

ERTÉ'S FASHION DESIGNS, Erté. 210 black-and-white inventions from *Harper's Bazar*, 1918-32, plus 8pp. full color covers. Captions. 88pp. 9 × 12. 24203-X Pa. $6.95

ERTÉ GRAPHICS, Erté. Collection of striking color graphics: *Seasons, Alphabet, Numerals, Aces* and *Precious Stones*. 50 plates, including 4 on covers. 48pp. 9⅜ × 12¼. 23580-7 Pa. $6.95

PAPER FOLDING FOR BEGINNERS, William D. Murray and Francis J. Rigney. Clearest book for making origami sail boats, roosters, frogs that move legs, etc. 40 projects. More than 275 illustrations. 94pp. 5⅜ × 8½. 20713-7 Pa. $2.25

ORIGAMI FOR THE ENTHUSIAST, John Montroll. Fish, ostrich, peacock, squirrel, rhinoceros, Pegasus, 19 other intricate subjects. Instructions. Diagrams. 128pp. 9 × 12. 23799-0 Pa. $4.95

CROCHETING NOVELTY POT HOLDERS, edited by Linda Macho. 64 useful, whimsical pot holders feature kitchen themes, animals, flowers, other novelties. Surprisingly easy to crochet. Complete instructions. 48pp. 8¼ × 11. 24296-X Pa. $1.95

CROCHETING DOILIES, edited by Rita Weiss. Irish Crochet, Jewel, Star Wheel, Vanity Fair and more. Also luncheon and console sets, runners and centerpieces. 51 illustrations. 48pp. 8¼ × 11. 23424-X Pa. $2.50

YUCATAN BEFORE AND AFTER THE CONQUEST, Diego de Landa. Only significant account of Yucatan written in the early post-Conquest era. Translated by William Gates. Over 120 illustrations. 162pp. 5⅜ × 8½.   23622-6 Pa. $3.50

ORNATE PICTORIAL CALLIGRAPHY, E.A. Lupfer. Complete instructions, over 150 examples help you create magnificent "flourishes" from which beautiful animals and objects gracefully emerge. 8⅛ × 11.   21957-7 Pa. $2.95

DOLLY DINGLE PAPER DOLLS, Grace Drayton. Cute chubby children by same artist who did Campbell Kids. Rare plates from 1910s. 30 paper dolls and over 100 outfits reproduced in full color. 32pp. 9¼ × 12¼.   23711-7 Pa. $3.50

CURIOUS GEORGE PAPER DOLLS IN FULL COLOR, H. A. Rey, Kathy Allert. Naughty little monkey-hero of children's books in two doll figures, plus 48 full-color costumes: pirate, Indian chief, fireman, more. 32pp. 9¼ × 12¼.
          24386-9 Pa. $3.50

GERMAN: HOW TO SPEAK AND WRITE IT, Joseph Rosenberg. Like *French, How to Speak and Write It*. Very rich modern course, with a wealth of pictorial material. 330 illustrations. 384pp. 5⅜ × 8½.   20271-2 Pa. $4.95

CATS AND KITTENS: 24 Ready-to-Mail Color Photo Postcards, D. Holby. Handsome collection; feline in a variety of adorable poses. Identifications. 12pp. on postcard stock. 8¼ × 11.   24469-5 Pa. $2.95

MARILYN MONROE PAPER DOLLS, Tom Tierney. 31 full-color designs on heavy stock, from *The Asphalt Jungle, Gentlemen Prefer Blondes*, 22 others. 1 doll. 16 plates. 32pp. 9⅜ × 12¼.   23769-9 Pa. $3.50

FUNDAMENTALS OF LAYOUT, F.H. Wills. All phases of layout design discussed and illustrated in 121 illustrations. Indispensable as student's text or handbook for professional. 124pp. 8⅛.× 11.   21279-3 Pa. $4.50

FANTASTIC SUPER STICKERS, Ed Sibbett, Jr. 75 colorful pressure-sensitive stickers. Peel off and place for a touch of pizzazz: clowns, penguins, teddy bears, etc. Full color. 16pp. 8¼ × 11.   24471-7 Pa. $3.50

LABELS FOR ALL OCCASIONS, Ed Sibbett, Jr. 6 labels each of 16 different designs—baroque, art nouveau, art deco, Pennsylvania Dutch, etc.—in full color. 24pp. 8¼ × 11.   23688-9 Pa. $2.95

HOW TO CALCULATE QUICKLY: RAPID METHODS IN BASIC MATHE-MATICS, Henry Sticker. Addition, subtraction, multiplication, division, checks, etc. More than 8000 problems, solutions. 185pp. 5 × 7¼.   20295-X Pa. $2.95

THE CAT COLORING BOOK, Karen Baldauski. Handsome, realistic renderings of 40 splendid felines, from American shorthair to exotic types. 44 plates. Captions. 48pp. 8¼ × 11.   24011-8 Pa. $2.50

THE TALE OF PETER RABBIT, Beatrix Potter. The inimitable Peter's terrifying adventure in Mr. McGregor's garden, with all 27 wonderful, full-color Potter illustrations. 55pp. 4¼ × 5½. (Available in U.S. only)   22827-4 Pa. $1.75

BASIC ELECTRICITY, U.S. Bureau of Naval Personnel. Batteries, circuits, conductors, AC and DC, inductance and capacitance, generators, motors, trans-formers, amplifiers, etc. 349 illustrations. 448pp. 6½ × 9¼.   20973-3 Pa. $7.95

SOURCE BOOK OF MEDICAL HISTORY, edited by Logan Clendening, M.D. Original accounts ranging from Ancient Egypt and Greece to discovery of X-rays: Galen, Pasteur, Lavoisier, Harvey, Parkinson, others. 685pp. 5⅜ × 8½.
20621-1 Pa. $10.95

THE ROSE AND THE KEY, J.S. Lefanu. Superb mystery novel from Irish master. Dark doings among an ancient and aristocratic English family. Well-drawn characters; capital suspense. Introduction by N. Donaldson. 448pp. 5⅜ × 8½.
24377-X Pa. $6.95

SOUTH WIND, Norman Douglas. Witty, elegant novel of ideas set on languorous Meditterranean island of Nepenthe. Elegant prose, glittering epigrams, mordant satire. 1917 masterpiece. 416pp. 5⅜ × 8½. (Available in U.S. only)
24361-3 Pa. $5.95

RUSSELL'S CIVIL WAR PHOTOGRAPHS, Capt. A.J. Russell. 116 rare Civil War Photos: Bull Run, Virginia campaigns, bridges, railroads, Richmond, Lincoln's funeral car. Many never seen before. Captions. 128pp. 9⅜ × 12¼.
24283-8 Pa. $7.95

PHOTOGRAPHS BY MAN RAY: 105 Works, 1920-1934. Nudes, still lifes, landscapes, women's faces, celebrity portraits (Dali, Matisse, Picasso, others), rayographs. Reprinted from rare gravure edition. 128pp. 9⅜ × 12¼. (Available in U.S. only)
23842-3 Pa. $7.95

STAR NAMES: THEIR LORE AND MEANING, Richard H. Allen. Star names, the zodiac, constellations: folklore and literature associated with heavens. The basic book of its field, fascinating reading. 563pp. 5⅜ × 8½.
21079-0 Pa. $7.95

BURNHAM'S CELESTIAL HANDBOOK, Robert Burnham, Jr. Thorough guide to the stars beyond our solar system. Exhaustive treatment. Alphabetical by constellation: Andromeda to Cetus in Vol. 1; Chamaeleon to Orion in Vol. 2; and Pavo to Vulpecula in Vol. 3. Hundreds of illustrations. Index in Vol. 3. 2000pp. 6⅛ × 9¼.
23567-X, 23568-8, 23673-0 Pa. Three-vol. set $36.85

THE ART NOUVEAU STYLE BOOK OF ALPHONSE MUCHA, Alphonse Mucha. All 72 plates from *Documents Decoratifs* in original color. Stunning, essential work of Art Nouveau. 80pp. 9⅜ × 12¼.
24044-4 Pa. $7.95

DESIGNS BY ERTE; FASHION DRAWINGS AND ILLUSTRATIONS FROM "HARPER'S BAZAR," Erte. 310 fabulous line drawings and 14 *Harper's Bazar* covers, 8 in full color. Erte's exotic temptresses with tassels, fur muffs, long trains, coifs, more. 129pp. 9⅜ × 12¼.
23397-9 Pa. $6.95

HISTORY OF STRENGTH OF MATERIALS, Stephen P. Timoshenko. Excellent historical survey of the strength of materials with many references to the theories of elasticity and structure. 245 figures. 452pp. 5⅜ × 8½.   61187-6 Pa. $8.95

Prices subject to change without notice.

Available at your book dealer or write for free catalog to Dept. GI, Dover Publications, Inc., 31 East 2nd St. Mineola, N.Y. 11501. Dover publishes more than 175 books each year on science, elementary and advanced mathematics, biology, music, art, literary history, social sciences and other areas.